HONG KONG

CONDENSED

KU-541-099

dani valent

LONELY PLANET PUBLICATIONS
Melbourne • Oakland • London • Paris

contents

Hong Kong Condensed
1st edition – January 2001

Published by
Lonely Planet Publications Pty Ltd
ABN 36 005 607 983
90 Maribyrnong St, Footscray,
Victoria 3011, Australia

Lonely Planet Offices
Australia Locked Bag 1, Footscray, Vic 3011
USA 150 Linden St, Oakland, CA 94607
UK 10a Spring Place, London NW5 3BH
France 1 rue du Dahomey, 75011 Paris

Photographs
Many of the images in this guide are
available for licensing from Lonely Planet
Images. email: lpi@lonelyplanet.com.au
Images used with kind permission of Hong
Kong Tourist Association, Hong Kong
Museum of History and Siren Entertainment.

Front cover photographs
Top: Wong Tai Sin Temple (Richard I'Anson)
Bottom: Burning Incense (Lee Foster)

ISBN 1 86450 253 3

Text & maps © Lonely Planet 2001
Photos © photographers as indicated 2001

Printed by Colorcraft Ltd, Hong Kong

how to use this book

KEY TO SYMBOLS

⊠	address	↘	Hillside Escalator Link
☎	telephone number	ⓘ	tourist information
e	email/web site address	☉	opening hours
Ⓜ	nearest MTR (subway) station	⑤	cost, entry charge ($HK)
⚑	nearest ferry wharf	⛐	wheelchair access
⛛	nearest tram route	⚗	child-friendly
⬚	nearest bus route	✗	on-site or nearby eatery
⬚	nearest train station	Ⅴ	vegetarian, or with a good selection

COLOUR-CODING

Each chapter has a different colour code which is reflected on the maps for quick reference (eg all Highlights are bright yellow on the maps).

MAPS & GRID REFERENCES

The fold-out maps on the front and back covers are numbered from 1 to 7. All sights and venues in the text have map references which indicate where to find them; eg (2, C3) means Map 2, grid reference C3. All sights and many other items are marked on the maps. For items not marked, the street is marked.

PRICES

All prices in this book are in Hong Kong dollars ($HK; $ in this book). Price gradings (eg $100/25) usually indicate adult/concession entry charges. Concession prices can include child, pensioner and/or student discounts.

WARNING & REQUEST

Things change – prices go up, schedules change, good places go bad and bad places improve or go bankrupt. So, if you find things better or worse, recently opened or long since closed, please tell us and help make the next edition even more accurate. Everyone who writes to us will find their name and possibly excerpts from their correspondence in one of our publications (let us know if you *don't* want your letter published or your name acknowledged). They will also receive the latest issue of *Planet Talk*, our quarterly printed newsletter, or *Comet*, our monthly email newsletter. Subscriptions to both newsletters are free. The very best contributions will be rewarded with a free guidebook.

Send all correspondence to the Lonely Planet office closest to you (p. 123).

Lonely Planet books provide independent advice. Lonely Planet does not accept advertising in guidebooks, nor payment in exchange for listing or endorsing any place or business. Lonely Planet writers do not accept discounts or payments in exchange for positive coverage of any sort.

facts about hong kong

This is Hong Kong: your mobile phone rings while you're shopping for dried fish stomach at a cluttered stall shadowed by a gleaming skyscraper. Or: you're eating bird's nest soup next to a woman wearing a chic anti-pollution face mask, a cutesy hair-bow and a T-shirt that reads 'Hysteric Glamour'. This is Hong Kong too: you're heading upstairs with a stomach full of tea and cake when the concierge glides up to say your suit is ready for the second fitting. And later: you're celebrating the closing of a deal with colleagues at a seafood restaurant with a prime harbour view and you're managing the chopsticks like a professional.

Hong Kong has the big city specials like smog, odour, 14 million elbows and an insane love of clatter. But it's also efficient, hushed and peaceful: the transport network is excellent, the shopping centres are sublime and the temples and quiet corners of parks are contemplative oases.

It's an intoxicating place, spectacular, exotic and accessible. The food is fantastic, the shopping is great, there are some terrific hotels, doing business is a breeze and there's a surprising range of nature-loving getaways within easy reach. If you're visiting for business, you'll find pleasure sneaking up on you; if you're visiting for pleasure, there are thousands of locals who make it their business to please.

Brash and hectic up close, Central sparkles coolly at twilight across Victoria Harbour.

HISTORY

Before Britain claimed Hong Kong, it was a neglected corner of the Qing dynasty (1644-1911) empire inhabited by farmers, fishermen and pirates. Trade between China and Britain commenced in 1685 but the balance was in favour of China until the British started trading opium to the Chinese in the late 18th century.

Chinese Emperor Dao Guang soon banned opium but illegal trade continued until 1839, when mandarin Lin Zexu destroyed 20,000 chests of the 'foreign mud'. British Foreign Secretary Lord Palmerston ordered his navy to force open the closed doors of Chinese trade. The British blockaded Guangzhou and then sailed north, forcing the Chinese to negotiate. Captain Charles Elliot, the chief superintendent of trade, demanded that a small, hilly island near the Pearl River estuary be ceded 'in perpetuity'. As Elliot saw it, this could be the British Empire's permanent outpost in the Far East.

Hong Kong formally became a British possession on 26 June 1843. The Second Anglo-Chinese War in 1860 gave the British the Kowloon peninsula, and 40 years later they also claimed the New Territories. Instead of annexing the land outright, they agreed to a 99-year lease. The countdown to British Hong Kong's expiration had begun.

Steady numbers of Chinese refugees entered the colony during the 1920s and 30s, but in 1941 Japan swept into Hong Kong and occupied the territory for four years.

The communist revolution in 1949 sent refugees pouring into Hong Kong and the city was reinvented as an immense manufacturing and financial centre. By the end of the 1950s Hong Kong-made textiles, watches and basic electronics had turned the colony into an unlikely economic powerhouse. From 600,000 people in 1945, Hong Kong's population soared to three million in 1960.

China was not a shy and retiring neighbour. In 1962 it opened the border gates, allowing 70,000 people to flood into the colony in a few weeks. In 1967, at the height of the Cultural Revolution, riots inspired by the Red Guards rocked the colony. Panic spread but Hong Kong's colonial masters

Land Grab Gag

'Albert is so amused at my having got the island of Hong Kong', wrote Queen Victoria to King Leopold of Belgium in 1841. While her husband could see the funny side of this apparently useless little island off the south coast of China Lord Palmerston was less amused. He considered the acquisition of Hong Kong a massive bungle. 'A barren island with hardly a house upon it!' he raged in a letter to the man responsible for the deal, Captain Charles Elliot.

A Chinese junk sails past the barren little island that was Hong Kong.

held their ground, police gradually restored order and Hong Kong got on with the business of getting rich.

During the 1970s, Taiwan, South Korea and Singapore began to mimic Hong Kong's success. Just as their cheap labour was threatening to undermine Hong Kong manufacturers, China under Deng Xiaoping opened up the country to tourism and foreign investment. Trade in Hong Kong skyrocketed as it became a transshipment point for China.

Few people gave much thought to Hong Kong's future until the early 1980s, when the British and Chinese governments started meeting to decide what would happen come 1997. Though Britain was legally bound to hand back only the New Territories, it would have been an awkward division. In December 1984 the British formally agreed to hand back the entire colony in 1997. A joint declaration theoretically allowed the 'Hong Kong Special Administrative Region (SAR) of China' to retain its social, economic and legal systems for at least 50 years after 1997. In 1988 Beijing published the Basic Law for Hong Kong, enshrining rights to property, travel, trade and free speech.

Though China insists that the Basic Law is the Hong Kong people's guarantee of the good life,

Facts & Figures
- Population — 6.9 million
- No. of Filipino maids — 140,000
- Office space costs up to $75,347/sq m
- Household income av. — $216,000/yr
- Land reclaimed from sea — 62 sq km
- Hotel rooms available — 35,000
- No. of tourists (1999) — 10.6 million
- Av. tourist length of stay — 3.2 nights

There's 6900 people for every HK sq km.

Beijing's actions since have given Hong Kongers cause to worry. Chief among these was the Tiananmen Square massacre of 4 June 1989 after which confidence plummeted in Hong Kong and capital headed overseas.

In 1996 Beijing-led elections were held for the position of Chief Executive, a new leadership position created under the Basic Law. Shipping tycoon Tung Chee Hwa was the predictable choice: he's the acceptable face of China to Hong Kong, being a speaker of Cantonese and English, and an expert businessman.

As the handover drew near, panic gave way to pragmatism. On the night of 30 June 1997, the last governor, Chris Patten, sailed away, the new rulers perused their domain and the expected political storm didn't eventuate.

Questions of political and social stability aside, Hong Kong was embroiled in the financial chaos that besieged South-East Asia in 1998. Though not as robust as it has been, Hong Kong is still a vibrant financial centre and one of the world's great cities. China has adopted a sensible hands-off policy that is working well. As long as Hong Kong carries on making money and making little noise, it is thought that Beijing will be content to leave things alone.

ORIENTATION

Hong Kong is comprised of Hong Kong Island (78 sq km) to the south, the mainland peninsula of Kowloon (12 sq km) to the north, and the New Territories (980 sq km) which sprawl north to mainland China. Hong Kong's 260 islands are also part of the New Territories. Surprisingly, a good deal of Hong Kong is mountainous and sparsely inhabited. Around 40% of the territory is dedicated country parks.

The city itself is centred around Victoria Harbour, comprising the northern strip of Hong Kong Island and southern Kowloon. The main business district is Central, on Hong Kong Island. East of Central lies the Admiralty commercial district, and then Wan Chai, known for restaurants and clubs. Next along is Causeway Bay, a major shopping area. East of Causeway Bay the mix becomes residential/industrial. Towering above it all is the Peak, an exclusive residential district.

On the Kowloon side, Tsim Sha Tsui, Jordan and Yau Ma Tei are busy hotel and shopping areas, while Mong Kok, north of Yau Ma Tei, is a bustling residential and local shopping area. See pages 32-4 for more detail.

Harbour nights, harbour lights

ENVIRONMENT

It's only in the last decade that Hong Kong authorities decided to do something about their territory becoming a densely populated cesspool. The fledgling Environmental Protection Department has to deal with decades of serious environmental abuse and a population which hasn't been educated about the implications of casual littering and pollution.

Hong Kong's waterways and air are terribly polluted. Victoria Harbour has been treated as a sewer while smoke-belching factories, ceaseless construction and large numbers of diesel vehicles have made the air a misery to breathe. Animals that have survived, such as pink dolphins and protected birds, are struggling.

Not all of Hong Kong is ravaged though: 21 country parks are protected from development, and all 17 reservoirs lie within their boundaries. Other positive signs include campaigns against littering and pollution, the monitoring of beaches for disease-causing bacteria and the introduction of some electric buses. However, these are minor initiatives given the 14,240 tonnes of municipal waste and 29,000 tonnes of construction waste generated *each day* in Hong Kong.

GOVERNMENT & POLITICS

The overarching framework is Beijing's Basic Law, which bestows freedom on Hong Kong except in foreign affairs. But Hong Kong is not politically

Hong Kong Tourist Association

Lawmaker's lair: the Legislative Council

democratic, nor has it ever been. Business governs the territory, the democratic elements that exist are limited and the people are largely apolitical.

The executive branch of power is led by the Chief Executive, who is supported by an Executive Council. The Chief Executive is further supported by a Financial Secretary, responsible for the economic policies of the government and the Secretary for Justice, responsible for drafting legislation.

The Legislative Council makes and debates laws and controls public expenditure. An independent judiciary administers justice and interprets the law.

The Urban and Regional Councils and District Boards are in charge of the day-to-day running of services including garbage collection and public recreation. Some of their representatives are elected.

Post-colonial Hong Kong has subtly changed. The territory has become more executive-led, turning the Legislative Council into little more than a rubber stamp. Furthermore, the civil service is becoming less accountable, prompting fears that the corruption that dogged it in the past will return.

ECONOMY

Business is Hong Kong's heart and soul. Despite the economic catastrophe of late 1997, Hong Kong is still a capitalist's dream: free enterprise and free trade, very low taxes, a hard-working labour force and excellent telecommunications. Personal income tax is a flat 15%, and the corporate profits tax is capped at 16.5%.

Service industries employ more than 75% of Hong Kong's workforce and make up nearly 80% of its GDP. Much of the services sector is underpinned by trade; Hong Kong is the world's eigth largest trading entity.

China is Hong Kong's largest partner, supplying the territory with around 33% of its total imports, and taking about 33% of its exports. The USA, Japan, Germany and the UK are also large markets.

Hong Kong maintained average GDP growth of around 5% through the 1990s. While enviable, this has kept inflation high, with an annual rise in the cost of living of about 7%. Recently, however, property prices and rents (including hotel rates) have dropped considerably.

SOCIETY & CULTURE

While Hong Kong is very westernised, Chinese beliefs and traditions dominate. Buddhism and Taoism are the main religions, though Confucianism, ancestor worship and ancient animist beliefs have been incorporated into the milieu (in addition to Christianity, Islam, Hinduism and other faiths). On a daily level the Chinese are much less concerned with high-minded philosophies than they are with the pursuit of worldly success, the appeasement of the dead and the spirits, and the seeking of hidden knowledge about the future.

Religion, superstition and traditional practices such as fung shui all come into play when trying to influence the course of fortune. Visits to temples are usually made for specific issues such as a relative's health, family prosperity or the success of a business.

Lucky Numbers

Many words share the same pronunciation in Cantonese, differing only in vowel tone. This has given rise to superstitions, especially when it comes to numbers. The number 3 sounds similar to 'life', 9 like 'eternity' and the ever-popular number 8 like 'prosperity.' Unlucky 4 has the same pronunciation as 'death'.

People love anything with an 8 in it: they'll pay more for an address that contains an 8 and August is the busiest month for marriages. Though most people don't worry too much about number 4, some buildings are missing their 4th floors and horse No 4 is often the least favoured in the race.

Fortune Telling The most popular method of divination in Hong Kong is using 'fortune sticks'. The altar of a temple, whether Buddhist or Taoist, is usually flanked by stacks of the wooden sticks (*chim*), which are housed in bamboo canisters. The routine is to ask the spirits or gods a question and shake the canister until one stick falls out. Each stick bears a numeral, which corresponds to a printed slip of paper in a set held by the temple keeper. That slip of paper should be taken to the temple's fortune-teller, who can interpret its particular meaning for you.

Fung Shui Literally meaning 'wind-water', *fung shui* aims to balance the elements of nature to produce a harmonious, prosperous environment. It's been in practice since the 12th century AD, and continues to play a role in the design and construction of buildings, highways, parks, tunnels and grave sites. Not everyone believes in fung shui, but few dare flout its dictates.

To guard against evil spirits, who can only move in straight lines, doors to the outside will sometimes be positioned at an angle. For similar reasons, beds cannot face doorways. Ideally, homes and businesses should have a view of calm water, but in the

Fung shui wheel of fortune

Hong Kong Tourist Association

absence of a sea view, a fish tank will do. Corporate heads are not supposed to have offices that face west: otherwise their company profits will go the same direction as the setting sun. Houses often have small fung shui objects placed strategically around the rooms. It is common to see two little dragons coiled up on the floor opposite the door, or two small golden lions looking out of the windows.

Chinese Zodiac

It is said that the animal year chart originated when Buddha commanded all the beasts of the earth to assemble before him. The names of the years were established according to the first 12 animals' order of arrival. There's no cat year as the rat tricked the cat into arriving late.

Your Chinese zodiac sign is based on the year of your birth. Being born or married in a particular year is believed to determine one's fortune so in this era of modern birth-control techniques, Chinese parents often plan for their children's sign. The year of the dragon (2000) sees the biggest jump in the birth rate, closely followed by the year of the tiger (1998).

Behold the mighty force of grey power!

Taijiquan

This form of slow motion shadow-boxing has been popular in China for centuries. It is basically a form of exercise, but it's also a martial art. *Taijiquan* (literally 'fist of the supreme ultimate') is very popular among older folk. The movements are supposed to develop the breathing muscles, promote digestion and improve muscle tone. It seems to work: there are some pretty sprightly old men and women out there.

Etiquette

Though fashion is taken seriously in Hong Kong, you can go to most restaurants and bars in casual dress. Even The Peninsula allows high-tea drinkers to wear jeans and sports shoes. This relaxed attitude does not extend to the business world, where dark suit and tie or conservative skirt and shirt rule supreme.

If you visit someone's home, it's best to bring a gift such as fruit, chocolate, brandy or whisky.

Beach-goers should note that nude or topless sunbathing is considered rude and offensive.

The Chinese are quite casual when it comes to table manners, but there are some dining rules that should be observed (see p. 68).

Business Card Manners

In Hong Kong's commercial circles, a business card is even more important than a nice suit. People simply won't take you seriously unless you have one. It's considered respectful to offer and accept cards using both hands. Bilingual cards can be printed within 24hrs; try printers along Man Wa Lane, Central or ask your hotel to direct you.

ARTS

Mention art in relation to Hong Kong, and the term 'cultural desert' will likely soon grace the conversation. It's not an altogether fair description. Granted, in a city where people will proudly declare that making money is the most important thing in life, the arts tend to take a back seat. But the arts still flourish in Hong Kong.

Architecture Architecture enthusiasts will find Hong Kong Island's Central and Wan Chai districts a fascinating showcase for the modern and postmodern. The Bank of China Tower, the Hongkong and Shanghai Bank Building, the Lippo Centre, Exchange Square, the Convention and Exhibition Centre and The Center are all impressive and very photogenic.

Progress has been made at the expense of history. About the only examples of pre-colonial Chinese architecture left in urban Hong Kong are the Tin Hau Temple in Tin Hau (near Causeway Bay) and the village house at the Law Uk Folk Museum in Chai Wan. There are walled villages, fortresses and 18th-century temples in the New Territories.

Colonial architecture is also in short supply. Most of what is left can be found on Hong Kong Island, including the Legislative Council building and the Museum of Medical Science in the Mid-Levels.

Dance One Chinese tradition that lives on in Hong Kong is the lion dance. A group of dancers/martial artists takes position under an elaborately painted costume of a mythical Chinese lion. To the accompaniment of blazing firecrackers and banging cymbals, the lion leaps around the crowd, giving the dancers a chance to demonstrate their acrobatic prowess.

There are three professional dance companies in Hong Kong. The Hong Kong Dance Company focuses on Chinese traditional and folk dances. The City Contemporary Dance Company stages modern dance. The Hong Kong Ballet performs both classical and modern pieces.

Film Hong Kong's reputation for churning out mindless action flicks, nonsense comedies and sickening romances has taken a battering in the last decade. Good stereotype-stomping films include *Rumble in the Bronx* (a better-than-average action starring Jackie Chan), *Farewell My Concubine* (about a Chinese opera troupe) and *Chungking Express* (love, obsession and a bewitching soundtrack). See p. 88 for more about Hong Kong film.

The annual Hong Kong International Film Festival brings in hundreds of films and is now one of the world's major film festivals.

Another Jackie Chan smash hit

Music Classical music is alive and well in Hong Kong. The city boasts a Chinese orchestra, as well as a philharmonic, sinfonietta and chamber orchestra. Overseas performers of world repute frequently make it to Hong Kong, especially during February's Hong Kong Arts Festival.

Cantopop dominates the popular music scene (see p. 91).

Theatre Nearly all theatre is Western in form, but most productions are staged in Cantonese and often provide an insightful look at contemporary Hong Kong life.

The Hong Kong Repertory Theatre tends towards larger scale productions of original works on Chinese themes and translated Western plays. Actors in many of the local companies are graduates of the Hong Kong Academy for Performing Arts, which also stages some interesting student shows.

English-language theatre in Hong Kong is mostly the domain of expatriate amateurs. See p. 87 for venue information.

> ### Chinese Opera
>
> Chinese opera is a world away from the Western variety. It is a mixture of singing, speaking, mime, acrobatics and dancing that last six hours.
>
> The main types of Chinese opera performed in Hong Kong are Beijing and Cantonese (see p. 87). Beijing opera is highly refined, using traditional props and almost no scenery. Cantonese is more like music hall theatre with 'boy meets girl' themes.
>
> Costumes, props and body language reveal much of the meaning in Chinese opera – the HKTA's *Hong Kong's Musical Heritage – Chinese Opera* handout makes things easier to understand and enjoy.

Kowloon Park art

Painting & Sculpture Painting in Hong Kong falls into three broad categories: modern local, classical Chinese and Western. Local artists often blend east and west, but some work in Chinese disciplines such as calligraphy and formal landscapes. The Museum of Art is quite strong on classical, but weak on contemporary art. As it develops, the new Heritage Museum may pick up the contemporary art mantle. At the moment, the most interesting art is in small private galleries (see pp. 39-40).

Many flagship properties are adorned with prestigious sculptures. Exchange Square has Henry Moore's *Oval with Points*, and *Taiji* by Taiwanese artist Zhu Ming. Facing Jardine House is *Double Oval*, also by Henry Moore. Inside the Mandarin Oriental Hotel are two copper reliefs by noted Chinese artist Cheung Yee. In Tsim Sha Tsui, near the Hong Kong Cultural Centre, stands *The Flying Frenchman* by Cezar. There are pieces by local artists at Kowloon Park's Sculpture Walk.

highlights

The best thing about being in Hong Kong is being in Hong Kong. It's about soaking up the atmosphere, being buzzed by the energy, getting flummoxed and fired by the confluences and contradictions of a Chinese city with multi-Asian and Western elements. It's about savouring new tastes, threading your way through human gridlock and realising you're humming some dumb Cantopop tune as you slurp your noodles.

Bona fide sights aren't exactly where it's at: there's no Eiffel Tower, no Met, no Forbidden City. Once you've been up the Peak and crossed the harbour on a ferry, you've pretty much done the must-dos. But while you're picking off our other highlights, you're sure to hit upon some of the random greats that make Hong Kong the exuberant delight that it is.

Lowlights

Hong Kong is not the easiest place to bumble around. For a start, no one here mooches: they're all hurrying with intent in their eyes. And it's an elbows-out, unapologetic kind of hustle. The air is filthy: there's nothing very charming about hacking up black gunk at the end of a day out and about. And if you want us to get even more petty and picky: the contemporary art galleries at the Hong Kong Museum of Art are a poorly curated joke; we're sick of air-conditioners dripping on our heads as we walk down the street; and once, just once, it would be nice to get a seat on the MTR.

Stopping Over?

One Day Catch a tram up the Peak for a good gawk at the city. Stretch your legs on a summit circuit before lunching at the Peak Café. Return to sea level for some shopping at Pacific Place. Watch the sun go down from Cyrano's, the Island Shangri-La bar.

Two Days Take the Star Ferry to Tsim Sha Tsui and visit the Art, Space or History museums. Have a yum cha brunch at Wan Loong Court in the Kowloon Hotel, then browse Nathan Rd until you're hungry enough for afternoon tea at The Peninsula. Wander up Temple St for the night market, snacking on street food as the need arises.

Three Days Explore Central and Sheung Wan, poking your head into traditional shops before lunching and gallery-hopping in Soho. Take a tram to Wan Chai for a night of Chinese opera or theatre at the Arts Centre. Strut your stuff at a Wan Chai bar before dining late at 369 Shanghai.

Is the sky the limit? If the skyline is any indication, Hong Kong is booming along.

Hong Kong Tourist Association

HAPPY VALLEY RACECOURSE   (5, J2)

Apart from mahjong games and the Mark Six Lottery, racing is the only form of legal gambling in Hong Kong. The first horse races were held in 1846 at Happy Valley Racecourse and became an annual event. Now there are about 75 meetings a year split between Happy Valley and the newer, larger track at Sha Tin in the New Territories. The racing season runs from September to June with most races on Wednesday nights.

If you've been in Hong Kong for less than 21 days you can get a tourist ticket. This is worthwhile, especially when the racecourse is crowded – at times up to 50,000 fans have been turned away! Tourist ticket-holders will be admitted despite the crowds – you can also walk around next to the finish area. Bring your passport to qualify.

Racing buffs can wallow in history at the **Hong Kong Racing Museum** on the 2nd floor of the Happy Valley Stand at the racecourse – it's open throughout the year.

Also of historical interest are several cemeteries across Morrison Hill Rd. These are divided into Catholic, Protestant and Muslim sections and date to the founding of Hong Kong as a colony. The placement is somewhat ironic, as is Happy Valley's name, for the area was a malaria-infested bog that led to a fair number of fatalities before the swamps were drained. Many of the victims of the huge fire at Happy Valley Racecourse over 80 years ago are also buried there.

INFORMATION

- ✉ Wong Nai Chung Rd, Happy Valley
- ☎ 2966 7940
- 🚇 Happy Valley
- 🚌 1, 5a
- 🕐 Races: Sept-June, Wed 7-11pm & weekends as scheduled; Hong Kong Racing Museum: Tues-Sat 10am-5pm, Sun 1-5pm
- $ Races: $10-50; Museum: free
- ⓘ Hong Kong Racing Museum
- ☎ 2966 8065
- ♿ good facilities including toilets and dedicated seating
- ✕ food stands on site

Sport of Kings

Hong Kongers are passionate about the nags: the SAR has the highest per capita betting on horse races in the world with an annual turnover of $80 billion-plus.

An oasis for happy punters

BANK OF CHINA TOWER   (4, F7)

Still the architectural symbol of Hong Kong, this 74-storey building was completed in 1990. Impressive as it is, the building is very much a brash and hard-edged synopsis of the 1980s. The Bank of China building had to be bigger than the nearby Hongkong and Shanghai Bank building (see p. 21), as it represented the new power in town (the People's Republic of China) and did its best to dwarf the symbol of the exiting power (Great Britain). Though it's not the tallest building in town (that honour goes to Wan Chai's Central Plaza), the Bank of China still manages to dominate the skyline.

Lee Foster

INFORMATION

✉ 1 Garden Rd (cnr Murray Rd), Central

🚇 Admiralty/Central

🕐 Bank: Mon-Fri 9am-4.30pm, Sat 9am-12.30pm; Lobby: 24hrs

💲 free

♿ good

✕ LA Cafe (p. 96)

The interior of the building is ingeniously freed from the mass of structural supports. Weight-bearing columns are positioned in each of the four corners of the building, with a fifth running down the centre of the tower, but only to the 25th floor, from where it feeds into the four columns at each corner. This liberates space on each floor to benefit the work environment. The fabric and design of the support structures (steel and concrete) had to be built to withstand typhoon-intensity wind pressures.

Despite being designed by Chinese-born architect Ieoh Ming Pei, the building is clearly Western in inspiration. Chinese elements are incorporated but muted. The segments of the building rising upwards are claimed to be analogous to bamboo sections, but this metaphor is lost in the overall steel and glass composition; likewise, the angularity of the construction conflicts with the round form of natural bamboo.

Flanking the tower are two landscaped gardens that successfully pay allegiance to traditional Chinese aesthetics and add a natural dimension to the

Rubik's Diamond?
The puzzling asymmetry of the building is in reality a simple geometric exercise. Rising from the ground like a cube, it is successively reduced, quarter by quarter, until the south-facing quarter is left to rise ever upwards.

The staggered cutting off of each triangular column creates a prismatic allure.

Dennis Johnson

geometric display. A notable absence, for a building of this size, is the lack of Chinese lions by the main door.

The granite lobby is impressive and the banking hall on the third floor, with its vast marble floor, is illuminated by a 15-storey, light-filled atrium. Unfortunately the Bank of China, stranded as it is in a messy web of fly-overs, can't be accessed easily by pedestrians.

Many local Hong Kong Chinese see the building as a huge violation of the principles of fung shui. For example, the bank's four triangular prisms are negative symbols in the fung shui guidebook; being the opposite to circles, these contradict what circles suggest – money, perfection and prosperity. Furthermore, the huge crosses on the sides of the building suggest negativity and its shape has been likened to a praying mantis (unsur-prisingly, considered a threatening symbol), as the radio masts look like insect's antennae.

Even more sinister are the tri-angular angles on the surface of the building – these are associated with daggers or blades and it is claimed they cut into neighbouring build-ings. One angle cuts across the for-mer governor's residence (which previously had enjoyed fung shui protection) and this was used by some superstitious souls to explain the run of bad luck that afflicted Chris Patten and his two predeces-sors in the governor's post.

Take the express lift to the 43rd floor from where you'll be reward-ed with a panoramic view over Hong Kong. From here you are about the same height as the Hongkong and Shanghai Bank Building. It's rather a pity that you aren't allowed to go any higher as it is exciting swaying with the wind at the top.

John Hay

An angular landmark from any angle

HONG KONG TRAMS (4 & 5)

Hong Kong's slowest and least flashy mode of public transport is arguably its most fun. The 163 tottering trams comprise the only double-deck tram-car fleet in the world and, though they don't have the star appeal of the harbour ferries, the trams are endearingly antiquated and doggedly handy.

INFORMATION

☎ 2559 8918
◉ Central/Sheung Wan/
Wan Chai/
Causeway Bay
⛴ Star Ferry
🕐 6am-1am
💲 $2/1
ℹ see p. 109

The first trams got going in 1904, running across the north of Hong Kong Island from Kennedy Town to Shau Kei Wan. The network has been augmented by seven other routes over the decades, all of them passing through Sheung Wan, Central and Admiralty, and some sheering off to loop around Happy Valley Racecourse.

When the trams first started running they caused multiple sensations: the stops were packed with people but not all of them wanted to go anywhere. A great number just jumped on, walked through having a gander and treading on toes, then got off again, not quite game to ride. The trams were also delayed by hawkers who took advantage of the tramway by dragging their heavy carts along the well-made tracks – eventually in 1911, a law was passed banning carts with the same wheel gauge as the trams. This law is still in effect today.

Tram Trade

Nearly 300,000 passengers trundle along the 30km of track each day. Celebrity tram passengers have included Madonna, Sean Penn and Margaret Thatcher.

Even the trams are multi-storey affairs.

Thin, tall and terrific trams take tottering trips through town.

HONG KONG MUSEUM OF HISTORY

(3, E7)

Commercial Hong Kong has all eyes on the future but when you see a computer salesman tending the shrine in his shop, you get an inkling that much of the city's character lies in its past. To gain a deeper understanding of this intriguing city, you have to hang with its ancestors and get in the cupboard with its skeletons: thus a visit to this new museum (final stage to be completed mid-2001) is almost essential.

Purpose-built in Tsim Sha Tsui East next to the fun Science Museum, the history museum (formerly in Kowloon Park) takes the visitor on a fascinating walk through the area's past, from pre-historic times (about 6000 years ago, give or take a whisker) right through to the fast-talking present. Landform, climate, geology and flora and fauna are covered (some of the stuffed animals are looking a bit wonky) before the human stories get a look in. There are replicas of village dwellings, traditional Chinese costumes and a realistic re-creation of an entire street block from 1881, including an old Chinese medicine shop. There's a decent attempt to communicate the importance of folk culture.

The large collection of 19th- and early 20th-century photographs is very atmospheric but our favourite is the mosh of toys and collectibles from the 1960s and 70s when 'Made in Hong Kong' meant 'Christmas stocking trash'. Overall, the museum does a fine job of relaying the fascinating story of Hong Kong.

INFORMATION

- ✉ 100 Chatham Rd South, Tsim Sha Tsui East
- ☎ 2724 9042
- Ⓔ Tsim Sha Tsui
- 🚌 5c, 8
- ⊘ Tues-Sat 10am-6pm, Sun 1-6pm
- ⑤ $10/5 (free Wed)
- ⓔ www.lcsd.gov.hk/CE /Museum/History/
- ♿ good
- ✗ Fruit Shop (p. 81)

Hong Kong Museum of History

Hong Kong Museum of History

Hong Kong Museum of History

Hong Kong history in its brand new house.

DON'T MISS
- Ming Dynasty, Opium Wars and Japanese Occupation galleries
- handover displays • popping into the Science Museum next door

HONG KONG PARK (4, G7)

This is one of the most unusual parks in the world, deliberately designed to look anything but natural, and emphasising synthetic creations such as its fountain plaza, conservatory, aviary, artificial waterfall, indoor games hall, Visual Arts Centre, playground, viewing tower, museum and taijiquan garden.

For all its artifice, the park is beautiful in its own weird way and, with a wall of skyscrapers on one side and mountains on the other, makes for some dramatic photography.

INFORMATION

- ✉ Cotton Tree Dr, Admiralty
- Ⓜ Admiralty/Central
- 🚍 3, 12, 23
- 🕐 6.30am-11pm (conservatory & aviary 9am-5pm)
- $ free
- ♿ yes
- ✕ Pacific Place shopping centre (east of park, see p. 25)

Hong Kong Tourist Association

Perhaps the best feature of the park is the **aviary**. Home to more than 800 birds (and 30 different species), the aviary is huge. To enter is to have the impression of wandering into a world of birds. Visitors walk along a wooden bridge suspended about 10m above the ground and on eyelevel with the tree branches, where most of the birds are to be found.

Also in the park is the **Flagstaff House Teaware Museum** (p. 35). The building dates from 1846, making it the oldest western-style structure in Hong Kong. The most tranquil area of the park is the **taijiquan garden**. It's busiest early in the morning when locals come and do their exercises but at any time of day you're likely to find someone standing in a pose or sitting in restful silence.

Finally, a great parking spot in Hong Kong

Hong Kong Tourist Association

DON'T MISS
- steaming up in the conservatory • getting in a flap in the aviary
- checking out the Visual Arts Centre (see p. 40) • striking a pose in the taijiquan garden • letting the kids loose in the playground

HONGKONG & SHANGHAI BANK   (4, F6)

This 180m-tall building is a masterpiece of precision and innovation. The glass and aluminium structure is the fourth Hongkong Bank building at 1 Queen's Rd since the bank's founding in 1865. It cost nearly US$1 billion, making it the world's most expensive building when it was completed in 1985.

Locals call this place the 'Robot building', and it's easy to see why – it resembles one of those clear plastic models built so you can see how everything inside works. The gears, chains and motors of the escalators and lifts are all visible. The stairwells are only walled in with glass, affording dizzying views to workers inside the building. Structurally, the building is equally radical, built on a 'coat-hanger' frame.

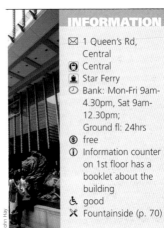

INFORMATION

- ✉ 1 Queen's Rd, Central
- Ⓒ Central
- 🚢 Star Ferry
- 🕐 Bank: Mon-Fri 9am-4.30pm, Sat 9am-12.30pm; Ground fl: 24hrs
- Ⓢ free
- ⓘ Information counter on 1st floor has a booklet about the building
- ♿ good
- ✗ Fountainside (p. 70)

This framework is a staggering achievement. The floor levels hang from five huge trusses supporting by eight groups of four-column steel clusters, wrapped in aluminium. Using this technique, British architect Norman Foster eliminated the need for a central core. If you stand in the light-filled atrium and look up, you can see how the whole structure hangs, rather than ascends.

The building makes concessions to fung shui orthodoxy: the escalators on the ground floor were positioned so as to maximise the flow of *qi* or *hei* (energy) into the building and the 1930s bronze lions (that guarded the doors of the previous Hongkong and Shanghai Bank building) were placed in a harmonious position.

Mirror Mirror
Hung on the south side of the building are 480 computer-controlled mirrors that reflect natural light into the atrium (it's called a sunscoop in architectural vernacular).

Flashy 80s meets exoskeletal industrial.

HONG KONG TRAIL   (2, D3)

Hong Kong has a truly surprising number of walking trails. For those who like a challenge, it is possible to tramp the length of Hong Kong Island on the rugged 50km-long Hong Kong Trail. Starting from the Peak Tram terminus on Victoria Peak, the trail follows Lugard Rd to the west, and drops down the hill to Pok Fu Lam Reservoir, near Aberdeen, before turning east and zigzagging across the ridges. The trail traverses four country parks: **Pok Fu Lam Country Park** south of Victoria Peak; **Aberdeen Country Park** east of the Peak; **Tai Tam Country Park** on the east side of the island; and **Shek O Country Park** in the south-east. Tai Tam is the largest of these parks, and arguably the most beautiful with its dense emerald forests and trickling streams. The Hong Kong Trail skirts the northern side of the Tai Tam Reservoir, which is the largest lake on the island.

Hong Kong Tourist Association

INFORMATION

🚌 Pok Fu Lam section:
   15 (from Exchange
   Sq to Victoria Peak);
   Tai Tam section: 6 or
   61 (from Exchange
   Sq to Wong Nai
   Chung Gap); Shek O
   section: see p. 51
💲 free
ℹ️ CPA ☎ 2422 9431;
   Government
   Publications Centre,
   66 Queensway,
   Admiralty ☎ 2537
   1910
🖳 www.afdparks.gov.hk
♿ toilets & accessible
   BBQs at visitors
   centre, Aberdeen
   Country Park
✘ Peak Café (p. 81)

It's possible to hike the entire trail in one day, but most walkers pick a manageable section to suit. For the spectacular **Dragon's Back** section of the trail see page 51 for the Shek O Excursion.

If you want to hike the trail, purchase the *Hong Kong Trail* map published by the Country & Marine Parks Authority (CPA). *Exploring Hong Kong's Countryside* by Edward Stokes is a useful book.

Richard I'Anson

Trail walkers are rewarded with spectacular urban and nature views.

DON'T MISS • 200 species of butterfly • frog-spotting • 500-year-old lichen in Pok Fu Lam • barking deer in the Tai Tam Valley

MAN MO TEMPLE   (4, D2)

This temple is one of the oldest and most famous in Hong Kong. The Man Mo (literally 'civil and military') is dedicated to two deities. The civil deity is a Chinese statesman of the 3rd century BC and the military deity is Kuanti, a soldier born in the 2nd century AD and now worshipped as the God of War. Also known as Kwan Tai or Kwan Kung, Kuanti's popularity in Hong Kong is probably more attributable to his status as the patron god of restaurants, pawn shops, the police force and secret societies such as the Triad organisations.

Outside the entrance are four gilt plaques on poles which are carried at procession time. Two plaques describe the gods being worshipped; the others request quietness and respect and warn menstruating women to keep away. Inside the temple are two antique chairs shaped like houses, used to carry the two gods at festival time. The coils suspended from the roof are incense cones burnt by worshippers. A large bell on the right is dated 1846 and the smaller ones on the left were made in 1897.

The exact date of the temple's construction has never been agreed on, but it's certain it was already standing when the British arrived to claim the island. The present Man Mo Temple was renovated in the mid-19th century.

Richard I'Anson

INFORMATION

- ✉ Cnr Hollywood Rd & Ladder St, Sheung Wan
- 🚌 26
- 🕑 8am-6pm
- 💲 free
- ✗ Rice Bar (33 Jervois St)

Wong Hotel

The area around the temple was used for location shots in the film *The World of Suzie Wong*, based on the novel by Richard Mason. The building to the right of the temple appears as Suzie's hotel, although the real hotel Luk Kwok (called Nam Kok in the film and now rebuilt) is in Wan Chai.

John Hay

A place of reflection for both civil and war-like types

NATHAN RD   (3, E5)

Kowloon's main drag was named after the governor, Sir Matthew Nathan, around the turn of the 20th century. It was promptly dubbed 'Nathan's Folly' since Kowloon at the time was sparsely populated and such a wide road was thought unnecessary. The trees that once lined the street are gone but some would say the folly has remained.

INFORMATION

- Tsim Sha Tsui/ Jordan/Yau Ma Tei/ Mong Kok
- Star Ferry
- 1, 1a, 2, 6, 6a, 7
- yes
- Avenue (p. 71; Holiday Inn Golden Mile, 50 Nathan Rd)

Richard Nebesky

From the waterfront all the way north to the New Territories border, Nathan Rd is packed with shops and hotels and people darting in and out of them. It's loud, crowded, relentless, intoxicating and, with dozens of buses juddering along its length, rather asphyxiating.

The lower end of the road is known as the **Golden Mile**, after both its real estate prices and its ability to suck money out of tourists' pockets. Seedy guesthouse ghettoes awkwardly rub shoulders with top-end hotels, Indian tailors ply their trade on street corners and every other person seems intent on divesting you of wads of cash. The seediest spot of all is **Chungking Mansions**, No 36-44, a squalid high-rise budget accommodation ghetto filled with

East and West bump shoulders on Nathan.

Richard l'Anson

equal parts backpacker and immigrant. It featured in Wong Kar-Wai's fantastic 1994 film *Chungking Express*. The HKTA would rather you focused on the Holiday Inn next door or the Hyatt Regency over the road, but Chungking and its ilk are genuine Hong Kong too.

Nathan Road's life in the past lane

DON'T MISS

- a drink at the Sheraton's Sky Lounge (No 20) • high fashion at Joyce Ma's (No 23) • Chinese goodies at Yue Hwa (No 143-161) • a detour into Kowloon Park • taking a double-decker bus back to the Star Ferry

PACIFIC PLACE (4, G9)

Designed and constructed by Wong & Ouyang Ltd and managed by the blue-chip Swire group, Pacific Place is an impressive feat of organised form.

In many ways it is typical of Hong Kong's large-scale commercial developments. However, the harmonies of shape and the originality of style reveal the architects' concern to produce novel solutions to the island's perennial problem of space.

Constructed in two phases, Phase I consisted of a huge podium for shops and cinemas (currently the UA Queensway cinema), topped by an office tower and the JW Marriot Hotel. The poetry comes from the harmonious outlines of the Phase II buildings (the Island Shangri-La and Conrad hotels), which soften the hard angles of Phase I and add beauty and balance to the complex. Against the predominantly squarish outline of Hong Kong architecture, the ellipses of the two Phase

INFORMATION

✉ 88 Queensway, Admiralty
☎ 2801 4197
🄼 Admiralty
🕐 24hrs (most shops open 10am-7pm)
ⓘ Information counter on L2
🄴 www.pacificplace.com.hk
♿ yes
✕ Yè Shanghai (p. 71)

Ordered retail madness

Trunk Talk

There's pampering aplenty in Admiralty's boutiques and hotels but the most coddled entity in the neighbourhood is a 120-year-old banyan tree. While Pacific Place was being built, about $24 million was spent on designing and constructing a concrete casing for the tree's roots, ensuring the happy coexistence of shopping centre and leafy lord. The noble if somewhat tortured specimen stands between the Conrad and Island Shangri-La hotels on Supreme Court Rd. It's accessible from the sixth floor of Pacific Place.

II buildings sneak grace and a skerrick of mystery into the crush of skyscrapers.

You don't have to be an architecture buff to enjoy shopping in Pacific Place. The mall is directly accessible from Admiralty MTR and has an excellent range of quality retail and food. Naturally, the major international and local brands are represented but there are a pleasing number of independent stores too. The complex is fairly easy to navigate and there are free telephones near the central elevators.

DON'T MISS • browsing Lane Crawford • coffee at Cova • miniatures at King & Country • measuring up at Pacific Place Tailors • a drink at Cyrano's in the Island Shangri-La

THE PENINSULA (3, J5)

More than a Hong Kong landmark, The Peninsula is one of the world's great hotels. Before WWII it was one of several prestigious hotels across Asia where anyone who was anyone stayed, lining up with the likes of the Raffles in Singapore and the Taj in Bombay.

INFORMATION

✉ Cnr Salisbury & Nathan Rds, Tsim Sha Tsui

☎ 2920 2888

🚇 Tsim Sha Tsui

⛴ Star Ferry

🕐 Afternoon tea: 2-7pm

💲 Afternoon tea: $165

e www.peninsula.com

♿ yes

🍴 Felix , Gaddi's (p. 78-9)

Unbeatable old world opulence

Glenn Beanland

Hong Kong Tourist Association

Land reclamation has robbed the hotel of its top waterfront location and the 20-storey extension is no architectural masterpiece, but the breathtaking interior is worth a visit and there are many reasons to linger.

Taking **Afternoon tea** at The Peninsula is one of the best experiences in town – dress neatly and be prepared to line up for a table. While you're waiting, you can listen to the string quartet and salivate at the sight of everyone else's cucumber sandwiches and dainty cakes. From 6pm, catch a dedicated lift up to the **Felix** restaurant, have a martini and gulp down the view. Stay for dinner or dress up for **Gaddi's**, the most exclusive French restaurant in town.

If you're dilly-dallying on luxury hotel accommodation, plunge into The Peninsula; there is a commitment to excellence that makes for a rare experience. See page 99 for more information.

THE PENINSULA

Hong Kong Tourist Association

A row of rollers waiting to whisk guests to and from the airport.

DON'T MISS • ordering a pot of fine tea • browsing the boutiques • asking to inspect one of the fab suites • using the men's loo at Felix (trust us)

REPULSE BAY (2, D3)

The pleasures of Repulse Bay don't lie in the water (murky), the seafloor (slimy) or the long, greyish beach. What Repulse Bay excels in is holiday atmosphere and people-watching, especially in summer when the beach is packed every day of the week.

Towards the eastern end of the beach is an unusual **Kwun Yum Temple**, popularly known as the Life Saver's Club. The temple area is full of statues and mosaics of Kwun Yum, the God of Mercy, and inside is the headquarters of the Royal Lifesaving Society. The sprawling temple houses an amazing assembly of deities and figures, including a four-faced Buddha and a posse of goats. Crossing the Longevity Bridge on the forecourt is supposed to add three days to your life (people walk back and forth to gain a month or two).

INFORMATION

🚌 6, 6a, 61
💲 free
🍴 Verandah (p. 77)

Rio it ain't, but it's far from repulsive.

You can keep walking east and south to **Middle Bay** and **South Bay**, respectively about 10 and 30mins walk along the shore. These beaches are usually less crowded but not any cleaner.

Repulse Bay is home to some of Hong Kong's rich and famous: the pink, purple and yellow condos with a giant square cut out of the middle are The Repulse Bay, also home to the fancy Verandah restaurant and an upscale shopping mall. Apparently this design feature was added at the behest of a fung shui expert, though such a stunt might also have been devised to push up the property's value.

DON'T MISS • walking along the beach • crossing the Longevity Bridge • afternoon tea at Verandah • watching couples pose for wedding photos

It's rare to find a quiet moment on the sand.

STAR FERRY   (3, K3)

Since 1898, gutsy double-decker ferries have chugged back and forth between Kowloon and Hong Kong Island. Over the decades land reclamation has made the journey marginally shorter, while rampant development has turned it into one of the most spectacular commutes imaginable. There's something nice about doing something on every tourist's A-list and finding that the gawping shutterbugs are outnumbered by blasé newspaper readers. Morning and evening, Star Ferries are a common way for the locals to hop from island to mainland and back again.

INFORMATION

- ☎ 2366 2576
- ⏱ 6.30am-11pm
- ⑤ $1.70/2.20 lower/upper deck (65 years of age and over free)
- ♿ yes
- ✕ City Hall Chinese Restaurant (p. 70)

John Hay

Though the ferries have names like *Morning Star*, *Evening Star* and *Celestial Star*, most of their traffic is through the starless daylight. It's at night though that the romance of the ferries comes to the fore: the boats are festively strung with lights, the city buildings beam an evening rainbow onto the rippling water, the energy of the day has eased and canoodling appears the only sensible thing to do.

There are four Star Ferry routes, but by far the most popular is the run between Tsim Sha Tsui and Central. The trip takes 7mins (they invite you to time it), and there are departures every 5 to 10mins.

Splash Ahoy

You must have exact change to pass through the turnstiles. If you need change, go to one of the staffed booths to gain entry. Be warned that the lower deck is susceptible to splashes and spray on gusty days – it's not 50c cheaper for nothing!

Richard I Anson

Not just another mode of public transport, the Star is a star attraction.

TEMPLE ST NIGHT MARKET   (3, C4)

Temple St (named after the Tin Hau Temple at its centre; see p. 37) is the liveliest night market in Hong Kong, and the place to go for cheap clothes, food, watches, pirate CDs, fake labels, footwear, cookware and everyday items. It used to be known as 'Men's St' because the market only sold men's clothing. Though there are still a lot of men's items on sale, vendors don't discriminate – anyone's money will do.

Any marked prices should be considered mere suggestions: this is definitely a place to bargain. You'll find the stall-holders tough negotiators though – keep in mind that HK$1 is worth around US10c if you're busting a gut over a couple of dollars.

INFORMATION

✉ Temple St,
   Yau Ma Tei
🚇 Yau Ma Tei/Jordan
🕐 6pm-midnight
   (best 8-11pm)
💲 free
♿ yes
🍴 Hing Kee (p. 83)

Richard I'Anson

Hong Kong Tourist Association

Worship at the temple of shop.

Haggle Gaggle

Say *pèhng didak m dak a?* (can you reduce the price?) to start negotiations. If the stall-holder stays high (they'll probably tap it in on a calculator) say *hó gwaih* (that's very expensive!) and see if they'll budge.

Does it exist if you can't buy it here?

Temple St extends all the way from Man Ming Lane in the north to Ning Po St in the south, and is divided by **Tin Hau Temple**. For street food, head to the section of Temple St north of the temple. You can get anything from a simple bowl of noodles to a full meal, served at your very own table on the street. There are also a few seafood and hotpot restaurants. Also on Temple St are all sorts of food stalls selling huge fried sausages *(heungcheung)* and fried kebabs with chicken *(gai)* and aubergine *(ayegwa)*. Do like the locals do: stand up and fortify yourself for the haggling ahead.

VICTORIA PEAK (2, C2)

First clear day, get your booty up here: if you haven't been to the Peak, then you haven't been to Hong Kong. Not only is the view one of the most spectacular cityscapes in the world, it's also a good way to get Hong Kong into perspective. Repeat the trip up on a not-too-murky night as the illuminated outlook is superb.

The Peak has been *the* place to live ever since the British moved in. The *taipans* (company bosses) built summer houses there to escape the heat and humidity (it's usually about 5°C cooler than down below). The Peak is still the most fashionable place to live in Hong Kong, as reflected by the astronomical real estate prices and bumper-to-bumper luxury traffic.

Anvil or wok on legs? Take your peak.

This being Hong Kong, there's a four-level shopping plaza plonked up here (the overblown, overpriced **Peak Galleria**) along with the **Peak Tower**, which resembles a huge titanium anvil and holds theme entertainment, shops, restaurants and the Peak Tram terminus.

When people refer to the Peak, they generally mean this plateau (400m elevation) and the surrounding residential area. Victoria Peak is actually the summit – about 500m to the west up steep Mt Austin Rd. The **old governor's mountain lodge** is near the summit (552m elevation). The lodge was burnt to the ground by the Japanese during WWII, but the gardens remain and are open to the public.

INFORMATION

- 🚋 Peak Tram, Garden Rd, Central (see p. 109)
- 🚌 15 (from Exchange Sq), minibus 1 (from Star Ferry)
- ⑤ free
- ⓘ Peak Tram ☎ 2522 0922; Ripley's Believe it or Not! odditorium ☎ 2849 0818
- ♿ yes (not tram)
- ✕ Peak Café, Café Deco and Restaurant Marché (see p. 81); also Cafe Victoria in the Peak Tower

You can walk around Victoria Peak without exhausting yourself. Harlech and Lugard Rds encircle it: Harlech Rd is on the south side while Lugard Rd is on the north slope and together they form a 3.5km loop. The walk takes about an hour and is lit at night. If you feel like a longer walk, you can continue for a further 2km along Peak Rd to Pok Fu Lam Reservoir Rd, which leaves Peak Rd near the car park exit. This goes past the reservoir to the main Pok Fu Lam Rd, where you can get the No 7 bus to Aberdeen or back to Central.

Another good walk is down to Hong Kong University (2, C1).

First walk to the west side of Victoria Peak by taking either Lugard or Harlech Rds. After reaching Hatton Rd, follow it down. The descent is very steep but the path is obvious.

The Peak is a good place to bring the kids: in the Peak Tower, there's the **Peak Explorer** (a futuristic ride in space and time), **Ripley's Believe it or Not! odditorium**, an outpost of Madame Tussaud's, the children-friendly Restaurant Marché and a viewing

I think I can, I think I can.

terrace with coin-operated binoculars. There are whispers that a bungy-jump will soon operate from the top of the anvil.

You should catch the **Peak Tram** at least one way. It's such a steep ride that the floor is angled to help standing passengers stay upright. Running for more than 100 years, the tram has never had an accident – a comforting thought if you start to have doubts about the strength of the cable. In 1885 everyone thought the Honourable Phineas Kyrie and William Kerfoot Hughes were crazy when they announced their intention to build a tramway to the top, but it opened three years later, wiping out the scoffers and the sedan-chair trade in one go. Since then, the tram has been stopped only by WWII and the violent rainstorms of 1966, which washed half the track down the hillside. The tram terminus is on Garden Rd, Central, at the north-west corner of Hong Kong Park, 650m from the Star Ferry terminal.

Taking a 'peak' is Hong Kong's number one tourist must-do.

DON'T MISS
• riding the Peak Tram • an ice cream on the viewing deck • walking to the top of the hill • jazz at the Peak Café • finding your hotel on the skyline

sights & activities

NEIGHBOURHOODS

Hong Kong Island

Though the island makes up only 7% of Hong Kong's land area, it is the territory's centre of gravity, and is home to most of the major businesses, government offices, top-end hotels and restaurants and upper-crust neighbourhoods. A great way to see the north side of the island is to jump on one of the wobbly double-decker trams. The south side, where the beaches are, has a completely different feel.

Away from the Tourists

If the tourist trail is getting you down, it's possible to get away from it all – even in manic Hong Kong. These lesser-known attractions are good spots to chill out:

- Chi Lin Nunnery (p. 37)
- CityU Gallery (p. 39)
- HK Heritage Museum (p. 35)
- Kowloon City Walled Park (p. 42)
- Lei Cheng Uk Museum & Han Tomb (p. 36)
- Victoria Park (p. 43)
- Tin Hau Temples (p. 37)

Aberdeen is rated as one of Hong Kong's top tourist attractions. The main lure is Aberdeen Harbour, where several thousand people still live aboard or work on anchored junks. The other main draw is a string of floating restaurants, Jumbo being the most famous (p. 77). To get really close to the action in the harbour, take a sampan tours. Sampan tours can be arranged at the Aberdeen Promenade (p. 53).

Just east of Central, **Admiralty** is a clump of office towers, hotels and shopping centres. There are no sights here, but the Pacific Place shopping mall is one of Hong Kong's nicest. You can connect to Hong Kong Park by taking the escalators up the west side of the mall, near the pedestrian bridge spanning Queensway. Across Queensway, the Lippo Centre makes an interesting addition to Hong Kong's skyline. Sitting on the hill above Pacific Place are the JW Marriot, Conrad and Island Shangri-La hotels, the main reasons why visitors make it to Admiralty.

Causeway Bay (along with Tsim Sha Tsui) is where Hong Kong goes to shop. Several shopping centres can be found south of Hennessy Rd, chief among them Times Square. If crowds bother you, steer clear of Causeway Bay on weekends. People also visit Causeway Bay to eat and, to a lesser extent, pub-crawl. The consumer rush gives this district a vibrant feel at almost any time of the day or night.

Nearly every Hong Kong visitor passes through **Central**, whether for sightseeing, taking care of business or en route to Lan Kwai Fong's bars and restaurants. Central also has some impressive architecture: historical remnants,

Hong Kong Tourist Association

Sitting on the dock of the Causeway Bay

skyscrapers, churches, and parks and gardens blend ancient and modern themes. The Star Ferry terminal is a good place to start exploring (p. 46). It's also the only place to get a glimpse of the city's last surviving rickshaws. West of the terminal, **Exchange Square** is ground zero for Hong Kong's business community.

Just uphill from the heart of Central, **Lan Kwai Fong** is a densely packed, pedestrian-only cluster of raucous bars and restaurants. The bars are nothing to get too excited about, but it's a fun place for a pub crawl. There are a number of good places to eat, too. At lunchtime during the week the district becomes a swirling mass of *chuppies* (Chinese yuppies) trying to squeeze a decent meal into a pitifully short lunch break.

Sheung Wan, just west of Central (to the right as you exit the Star Ferry), once had the feel of old Shanghai. The comparison is a bit forced now, since much of the old district has disappeared under the jackhammers of development but there are still tight-knit communities and shops that carry on business the same way they've done for decades. See page 47 for a neighbourhood walk.

Soho (SOuth of HOllywood Rd) is notable for its crush of restaurants, dishing up everything from Cajun to Manchurian. It's a lively place with galleries, *dai pai dongs* (open-air street stalls), antique stores, butchers and a nunnery. The restaurants are strung along Staunton and Elgin Sts west of the escalator.

One of Stanley's quieter moments

Stanley (the name in Cantonese means 'red pillar') is the trendy, suburban *gwailo* (foreigners') place to live. There are some great restaurants, the famous Stanley Market and a decent beach. It's on the south-east side of the island, just 15km as the crow flies from Central. See page 52 for a Stanley excursion.

Laundry day in Wan Chai

East of Central, **Wan Chai** ('little bay' in Cantonese) is one of Hong Kong's most famous enclaves. A seedy red-light district during the Vietnam War, Wan Chai remains an interesting place to explore. The area between Hennessy and Gloucester Rds has become a major entertainment district. Most of the hybrid bars, restaurants and clubs are clustered along Jaffe and Lockhart Rds, just west of the MTR station.

Kowloon

Strictly speaking, **Kowloon** is the 12 sq km extending from Tsim Sha Tsui north to Boundary St. Leave the glittering malls and hotels and you begin to see where Hong Kong and China converge, culturally at least. East doesn't really meet West in Kowloon, it swallows it up. Kowloon's districts are best seen on foot. There aren't too many fantastic sights; it's the overall experience that's worth taking in.

Mong Kok – jacket and tie not required

Mong Kok has one of the highest population densities of any place in the world, a point that hits home as soon as you arrive. Aside from housing a ridiculous number of people in shabby apartment blocks, Mong Kok is also one of Hong Kong's busiest shopping districts: the name in Cantonese aptly means 'prosperous corner'. This is where locals come to buy everyday items. The streets west of Nathan Rd, where you'll find many of the city's brothels, reveal Hong Kong's seamier side. See p. 48 for self-guided walk around the streets of Mong Kok.

Perched at the very edge of the peninsula, **Tsim Sha Tsui** (pronounced 'jim sa joy') is Hong Kong's tourist ghetto. Countless clothing and shoe stores, restaurants, pubs, sleazy bars, camera and electronics stores and hotels are somehow crammed into a small area. In behind The Peninsula hotel, around Ashley, Hankow and Lock Rds, is a warren of cheap (and often shady) shops, restaurants and bars. It's a fun area to wander around, particularly in the evening.

Hankow Rd, in crazy Tsim Sha Tsui

This triangular block of land east of Chatham Rd didn't even exist until 1980. Built entirely on reclaimed land, **Tsim Sha Tsui East** is a cluster of shopping malls, hotels, restaurants and nightclubs. The new History Museum is here, right next to the Science Museum. Everything is new – there are none of the old, crumbling buildings of nearby Tsim Sha Tsui.

Immediately north of Tsim Sha Tsui – and indistinguishable from it – is **Yau Ma Tei** (pronounced 'yow ma day'). In Cantonese Yau Ma Tei means 'place of sesame plants'. Today the only plants you'll find in this heavily urban district are in the window boxes of crumbling tenements. Yau Ma Tei's narrow byways are good places to check out Hong Kong's more traditional urban society. Within the square bordered by Kansu, Woosung, Nanking and Ferry Sts you'll stumble across pawnshops, outdoor markets, Chinese pharmacies, mahjong parlours and other retailers plying their time-honoured trades.

MUSEUMS

Flagstaff House Museum (4, F8)

The oldest western-style building still standing in Hong Kong (1846) houses a Chinese teaware collection. Pieces date from the Warring States period (473-221 BC) to the present. A gallery exhibits some rare Chinese ceramics and seals.

✉ Hong Kong Park (off Cotton Tree Dr), Central ☎ 2869 0690 ⊕ Admiralty ⊙ Thurs-Tues 10am-5pm ⑤ free ♿ yes

Fung Ping Shan Museum (2, C1)

This university museum houses ceramics and bronzes, plus a lesser number of paintings and carvings. The bronzes are in three groups: Shang and Zhou dynasty ritual vessels; decorative mirrors from the Warring States period to the Tang, Song, Ming and Qing dynasties; and Nestorian crosses from the Yuan dynasty. The ceramics collection includes Han dynasty tomb pottery and recent works from the pottery centres of Jingdezhen and Shiwan in China.

✉ HK University, 94 Bonham Rd, Western/ Kennedy Town ☎ 2859 2114 🚌 3 (from Edinburgh Pl) ⊙ Mon-Sat 9.30am-6pm ⑤ free

Hong Kong Heritage Museum (1, D7)

Housed in a mock-traditional building, this new museum (opened December 2000) has displays on Cantonese opera, a children's gallery with

Play spin the cannon at the Coastal Defence Museum.

toys on show and a gallery for the impressive art collection of Dr TT Tsui. Thematic galleries showcase anything from comics to woodblocks.

✉ 1 Man Lam Rd, Sha Tin ☎ 2180 8188 🚆 Sha Tin KCR ⊙ call for times ⑤ ♿ yes

HK Museum of Art (3, K5)

Part of the Cultural Centre complex, the Museum of Art does a good job with classical Chinese art, though there is a lack of background information to help the English-speaking visitor. The paintings and lithographs of old Hong Kong, and the Xubaizhi collection of painting and calligraphy are more easily digested. Another hall shows creditable international exhibitions, but the gallery falls down in contemporary art – visit the smaller galleries around for recent Chinese art. When your feet get sore, take a seat in the hallway and enjoy the harbour views.

✉ Cnr Salisbury & Nathan Rds, Tsim Sha Tsui ☎ 2734 2167 ⊕ Tsim Sha Tsui 🚢 Star Ferry ⊙ Fri-Wed 10am-6pm ⑤ $10/5 (free Wed) ♿ yes

Hong Kong Museum of Coastal Defence (2, C4)

The history of Hong Kong's coastal defence is presented in the recently restored 300-year-old Lei Yue Mun Fort. Exhibitions in the old Redoubt cover the Ming and Qing dynasties, the colonial years, the Japanese invasion and the resumption of Chinese sovereignty. There's a historical trail through casements, tunnels and observation posts.

✉ 175 Tung Hei Rd, Shau Kei Wan ☎ 2569 1500 ⊕ Shau Kei Wan (then 15mins walk north from B2 exit); Heng Fa Chuen (then free shuttle bus weekends and public holidays only) 🚌 84, 85, A12 ⊙ Fri-Wed 10am-5pm ⑤ $10/5 (free Wed)

Law Uk Folk Museum (2, C4)

Small and somewhat shabby, Law Uk has a high quotient of puppetry displays. The house on the grounds is a restored Hakka residence with simple but charming furniture and household items.

✉ 14 Kut Shing St, Chai Wan ☎ 2896 7006 ⊕ Chai Wan ⊙ Tues-Sat 10am-1pm, 2-6pm, Sun 1-6pm ⑤ free

BUILDINGS & MONUMENTS

Clock Tower (3, K3)
This 45m clock tower, built in 1922, is all that remains of the southern terminus of the Kowloon-Canton Railway (built in 1916 and torn down in 1978). The original building, which had columns and was in colonial style, was too small to handle the large volume of passenger traffic. See Hong Kong Cultural Centre below for details.

The towering timekeeper guards the Hong Kong Cultural Centre.

Exchange Square
(4, D6) Elevated above the fray, the square is the seat of the Hong Kong Stock Exchange. The huge statue in front of the Forum Mall is of a taijiquan posture known as 'Snake creeps down'. Ground level is given over to the bus station.
⊠ **Cnr Connaught Rd Central & Pedder St, Central** ⊖ **Central**
⚲ **Star Ferry**

Government House (4, F5)
The former residence of the governor dates back to 1858. The rectangular

tower was added by the Japanese during WWII. The current Chief Executive, Tung Chee-Hwa, turned down the offer to make it his abode, saying the fung shui wasn't satisfactory.
⊠ **Upper Garden Rd, Central** ⊖ **Central**
⊘ **closed to the public; open one Sun in Mar**

Hong Kong Convention & Exhibition Centre
(4, D12) This enormous complex boasts the world's largest 'glass curtain', a window seven storeys high. Expanded onto reclaimed land for the handover ceremony in June 1997, the extension reaches out into the harbour. The design of the extension is spectacular, symbolising a bird in flight (pop over to the Sky Lobby in Central Plaza for an overview).
⊠ **1 Expo Dr, Wan Chai** ☎ **2582 8888**
e **info@hkcec.com.hk**
⊖ **Wan Chai** ⛢ **tram**
⊟ **10a, 20, 21** ⊘ **9am-7pm (varies)** ⑤ **free (charges for some exhibitions)** ⅊ **yes**

Hong Kong Cultural Centre (3, K4)
The Cultural Centre is one of Hong Kong's landmarks. Within the tiled exterior, there's a 2100-seat concert hall, theatres, rehearsal studios, an arts library and an impressive main lobby. There are daily tours 12.30-1pm.
⊠ **Cnr Salisbury & Canton Rds, Tsim Sha Tsui** ☎ **2734 2009** ⊖ **Tsim Sha Tsui** ⚲ **Star Ferry** ⊘ **9am-11pm (Sun from 1pm)** ⑤ **free; tours $10/5** ⅊ **yes**

Jardine House (4, D6)
This 40-storey silver monolith is the HQ of Hong Kong's venerable conglomerate, Jardine Matheson. The building's porthole-style windows have earned it a less respectable Chinese nickname, which translates as 'Thousand Arseholes'. To the east of the building is Henry Moore's sculpture Double Oval.
⊠ **Cnr Connaught Rd Central & Pedder St, Central** ⊖ **Central**
⚲ **Star Ferry** ⊘ **Mon-Sat 7am-9pm** ⑤ **free**
⅊ **yes**

Lei Cheng Uk Museum & Han Tomb
(2, B2) This late Han dynasty (AD 25-220) burial vault was discovered in 1955 when workers were levelling the hillside for a housing estate. The tomb is encased in a concrete shell for protection and you can only peak through a plastic window.
⊠ **Lei Cheng Uk Estate, 41 Tonkin St, Cheung Sha Wan** ☎ **2386 2863** ⊖ **Cheung Sha Wan** ⊟ **2** ⊘ **Tues-Sat 10am-1pm, 2-6pm Sun 1-6pm** ⑤ **free**

Typhoon Shelter
(5, C3) The waterfront near here used to be a mass of junks and sampans huddling in the Causeway Bay Typhoon Shelter, but these days it's nearly all gwailo yachts. This should be no surprise, as the Royal Hong Kong Yacht Club is headquartered here.
⊠ **Victoria Harbour, Causeway Bay**
⊖ **Causeway Bay**

John Hay

PLACES OF WORSHIP

Chi Lin Nunnery
(2, A3) This Tang-style wooden complex is a serene place with lotus ponds, immaculate bonsai and silent nuns delivering offerings of fruit and rice to Buddha and deities. Built in 1998 using ancient techniques, the design is intended to demonstrate the harmony of humans with nature – it's convincing until you look up at the looming high-rises nearby.
✉ 5 Chi Lin Dr, Diamond Hill ☎ 2354 1882 ⊕ Diamond Hill ⏱ Thurs-Tues 9am-4pm

Kowloon Mosque & Islamic Centre
(3, G4) The present mosque (Hong Kong's largest) was completed in 1984 and occupies the site of a previous mosque (built in 1896) for Muslim Indian troops who were garrisoned in barracks at what is now Kowloon Park. The mosque, with its handsome dome, minarets and carved marble, is interesting to admire from the outside. Muslims are welcome to attend services but non-Muslims should ask if it's OK to look inside – remember to take off your shoes.
✉ 105 Nathan Rd, Tsim Sha Tsui ☎ 2724 0095 ⊕ Tsim Sha Tsui

St John's Cathedral
(4, F6) Built in 1847, this Anglican church is now lost in Central's forest of skyscrapers. Between 1942 and 1944 the Japanese Imperial Army used it as a social club and the building was ravaged. The wooden front doors were rebuilt after the war using timber salvaged from HMS *Tamar*, a British warship that guarded the entrance to Victoria Harbour. Behind the cathedral is the 1917 French Mission building, now home to Hong Kong's Court of Final Appeal.
✉ 4-8 Garden Rd, Central ☎ 2523 4157 e general@stjohns cathedral.org.hk ⊕ Central ⏱ 7am-6pm (plus daily services) ♿ yes

Tin Hau Temple, Yau Ma Tei
(3, A4) A few blocks north-east of the Jade Market, is a sizable temple dedicated to Tin Hau, the goddess of seafarers. The temple complex also houses an altar dedicated to Shing Wong God of the City and To Tei God of the Earth.
✉ Off Nathan Rd (btw Market & Public Sq Sts) ⊕ Yau Ma Tei ⏱ 8am-6pm

Tin Hau Temple, Causeway Bay
(1, G5) Just east of Victoria Park, this other Tin Hau Temple is tiny, and dwarfed by surrounding high-rises. Before reclamation, the temple to the seafarers' goddess stood on the waterfront. This has been a site of worship for 300 years, though the current structure is only about 200 years old.
✉ 10 Tin Hau Temple Rd (at Dragon Rd) ⊕ Tin Hau

> ### Lionising
> Just off to one side of the Wong Tai Sin Temple arcade is a small open area where you can get a magnificent view of Lion Rock, one of Hong Kong's prominent natural landmarks.

Wong Tai Sin Temple
(2, A3) This large, active Taoist temple was built in 1973. Like most Chinese temples, this one is an explosion of colour. Come in the late afternoon or early evening and watch hordes of devotees praying and divining the future with *chim* (sticks that must be shaken out of a box onto the ground and then read). Adjacent to the temple is an arcade populated by fortune tellers, some of whom speak good English. Behind the main temple are the Good Wish Gardens, replete with colourful pavilions, curved pathways and an artificial waterway.
✉ Adjacent Wong Tai Sin MTR, Wong Tai Sin ⊕ Wong Tai Sin ⏱ 7am-6pm

St John's – a church with a colourful past

HONG KONG FOR CHILDREN

The upside about bringing children to Hong Kong is that people are tolerant of child-caused chaos. Or, more accurately, restaurants, shopping centres and public transport are usually so noisy that no-one will blink if your toddler throws a tantrum. And the only good thing about Hong Kongers chatting through movies is that they probably won't care if your child forgets that silence is golden during a cinema session.

On the downside, the city is crowded and polluted, with a lack of public toilets and places where you can sit and gather yourself. There are playgrounds dotted here and there but there aren't many public parks where you can let the wild things exhaust themselves. That said, the colour and vibrancy of many of Hong Kong's sights will appeal to children.

Hong Kong Science Museum (3, F7)

The Science Museum is a multilevel complex with more than 500 displays on computers, energy, physics, robotics, telecommunications, health and more. Most exhibits are 'hands on', which helps to keep younger visitors interested. All in all it's a great place for kids and not a bad place for grown-ups to realise how interesting science classes could have been.
✉ 2 Science Museum Rd (near cnr Granville Rd), Tsim Sha Tsui East ☎ 2732 3232 ❷ Tsim Sha Tsui ⚓ HKF Hoverferry 🚌 5c, 8 ✆ Tues-Fri 1-9pm, Sat-Sun 10am-9pm ⑤ $25/12.50 ♿ yes

Ocean Park (2, D3)

Ocean Park (just south-east of Aberdeen) is a fully fledged amusement park, complete with a roller coaster and other stomach-turning rides. It is also something of a marine park, with daily dolphin and killer whale shows and a reef aquarium. There are also a couple of pandas. The two-part complex is linked by a scenic cable-car ride. The park entrance is on the 'lowland' side. The park's main section sits on the 'headlands' and affords a beautiful view of the South China Sea. At the rear is the Middle Kingdom, a sort of Chinese cultural village. This is a highly whitewashed version of ancient China, but it's harmless enough.
☎ 2552 0291 🚌 629 (from Central & Admiralty MTR); minibus 6 from Star Ferry terminal (Central) ✆ 10am-6pm ⑤ $140/70 ♿ yes

John Hay

Make some space for the kids.

Space Museum & Theatre (3, J5)

This peculiar, golf-ball shaped building is divided into three parts: the Hall of Space Science, the Hall of Astronomy and the Space Theatre planetarium. Exhibits include a lump of moon rock, models of a rocket ship and NASA's 1962 Mercury space

Babysitting & Childcare

Most hotels will be able to recommend a babysitter if you've got daytime appointments or want a night out *sans* child. Otherwise call **Rent-A-Mum** (☎ 2523 4868, rentamum@hknet.com), a reputable agency which supplies qualified English-speaking nannies for $95/hr.

John Hay

capsule. The Space Theatre screens 'sky shows' and IMAX films (daily except Monday), some in English and some in Cantonese.

✉ 10 Salisbury Rd, Tsim Sha Tsui ☎ 2734 9009 ⊕ Tsim Sha Tsui 🚢 Star Ferry ⏰ Museum: Mon, Wed, Fri 1-9pm, Sat-Sun 10am-9pm; Theatre: Tues-Sun 11.30am-8.30pm ⑤ Museum $10/5; Theatre shows from $24/12 ♿ yes

More Kiddie Attractions

As well as the sights listed here, children will most likely enjoy the **Yuen Po St Bird Garden** (p. 43), **Repulse Bay** (p. 27), the children's centre at the **Museum of Art** (p. 35), the animals in the **Zoological & Botanic Gardens** (p 42), the overpriced theme entertainment in the Peak Tower (p. 30) and the revolving restaurant in the Hopewell Centre (p. 69).

For less-structured activity, head to the playground in **Hong Kong Park** (p. 20) or for a wander past **Tung Choi St's goldfish shops** (near Bute St, Mong Kok; p. 48). Here you'll find a riot of colour and fishy movement. Hawkers sometimes sell big, fat bugs curbside here – very good for the gross-out factor.

GALLERIES

Alisan Fine Art (4, E6)
Contemporary expatriate and mainland Chinese painting, drawing and sculpture. The exhibits can be humdrum but Alisan still stands up as one of the first local galleries to promote mainland artists.
✉ Shop 315, Prince's Bldg, 10 Chater Rd, Central ☎ 2526 1091 e alisan@netvigator.com ⊕ Central 🚢 Star Ferry ⏰ Mon-Fri 10am-6pm, Sat 10am-5pm ⑤ free

Art Scene China (6, D5) This newcomer to the Hong Kong art scene aims to deliver contemporary mainland Chinese artists. The gallery represents established artists like Cao Li and Zhong Biao along with more recent ones, such as Ai An, He Sen and Song Hai Zeng.
✉ 1 Lan Kwai Fong, Lan Kwai Fong ☎ 2501 0211 e sami@aschina.com ⊕ Central ⏰ Mon-Sat 10.30am-7pm ⑤ free ♿ yes

CityU Gallery (2, A3)
Exhibitions in all media which often explore life in Hong Kong. Group shows include student and professional artists and are usually well curated.
✉ Amenities Bldg, 80 Tat Chee Ave, City University of Hong Kong, Kowloon Tong ☎ 2634 0339 ⊕ Kowloon Tong 🚌 2c ⏰ 10am-7pm ⑤ free

Fringe Club (6, E5)
The city's major alternative performance and exhibition space inhabits an old dairy at the edge of Lan Kwai Fong. Funding from the HK Arts Development Council enables the Fringe galleries to show challenging new work by local artists without an inordinate focus on

commercial viability.
✉ 2 Lwr Albert Rd, Lan Kwai Fong ☎ 2521 7251 e mail@hkfringe.com.hk; www.hkfringe.com.hk ⊕ Central ⏰ Mon-Thurs noon-midnight, Fri-Sat noon-2am ⑤ free ♿ yes

Galeriasia (6, D5)
Pan-Asian paintings, drawings and themed group shows. While you're in the building, have a look at **Galerie La Vong** (Vietnamese art) on the 13th floor (☎ 2869 6863).
✉ 6th fl, 1 Lan Kwai Fong, Lan Kwai Fong ☎ 2529 2598 e asianart@galerie asia.com ⊕ Central ⏰ 10.30am-7pm ⑤ free ♿ yes

Alisan: a fine art find

Galerie du Monde

(4, G9) Long-established upscale gallery showing mostly figurative work from relatively established mainland Chinese painters like Cheng Yuanan, Eng Tay and Pan Xun. There's a sideline in prints from Japan, Europe and the US. ✉ Shop 328, Pacific Place, 88 Queensway, Admiralty ☎ 2525 0529 e fineart@galeriedumonde.com 🚇 Admiralty ⏰ Mon-Sat 10am-7pm, Sun noon-5pm ⑤ free & yes

Galerie Martini

(6, D5) Small upstairs art nook which shows international contemporary art. The exhibitions swing between introducing relatively established Western artists to Hong Kong and giving exposure to local artists on the rise. ✉ 99f Wellington St, Soho ☎ 2526 9566 e galeriem@netvigator.com 🚇 Central ⏰ Tues-Sat 11am-7pm ⑤ free

HanArt TZ Gallery

(4, F6) One of the most influential and innovative galleries showing contemporary Chinese art with a thoroughbred stable of figurative and conceptual artists working in painting, sculpture and video. ✉ Henley Bldg, 5 Queen's Rd Central, Central ☎ 2526 9019 e tzchng@hanart.com 🚇 Central ⛴ Star Ferry ⏰ Mon-Fri 10am-6.30pm, Sat 10am-6pm ⑤ free & yes

Hong Kong Visual Arts Centre (4, G6)

Within the former Victoria Barracks, the centre comprises 10 studios and a modest exhibition space mostly showing ceramics, prints and sculpture produced on site. ✉ Hong Kong Park, 7a Kennedy Rd, Central ☎ 2521 3008 🚇 Central 🚌 3, 12, 12a; minibus 1a ⏰ Wed-Mon 10am-9pm ⑤ free

For striking visuals

John Batten Gallery

(6, C1) Small gallery charged with the enthusiasm and vision of its namesake director. Batten shows local and international painting, photography and video art of consistently good quality. ✉ 64 Peel St, Soho ☎ 2854 1018 e batten@asiaonline.net 🚇 Central ⏰ Tues-Sat 11am-7pm, Sun 1-5pm ⑤ free

OP Photo Gallery

(6, D2) Publicly funded photography gallery. Most of the work is local and will give you an alternative to glam and glossy Hong Kong happy snaps. ✉ 5 Prince St, Soho ☎ 2537 4716 🚇 Central ⏰ Wed-Sun noon-7pm ⑤ free

Pao Galleries (4, F11)

Major contemporary art gallery in the HK Arts Centre. Extending over two floors, there's room to host retrospectives and group shows in all visual media. The curatorial vision is lively without being too provocative. ✉ 2 Harbour Rd, Wan Chai ☎ 2582 0200 🚇 Wan Chai ⏰ 10am-8pm ⑤ free

Para/Site Art Space

(4, C1) Scrappily curated co-op space which is worth a look if you're wandering by. Most art on display is Chinese but there are occasional exhibitions by European and Australian artists. ✉ 3 Po Yan St, Sheung Wan ☎ 2517 4620 🚇 Sheung Wan ⏰ Wed-Sun noon-7pm (Thurs till 8pm) ⑤ free

Schoeni Art Gallery

(6, D2) Large gallery with a weird mix of modern Chinese art and antique furniture. Yue Min Jun is one of the heavyweight artists Schoeni represents. ✉ 21-31 Old Bailey St, Soho ☎ 2869 8802 e schoeni@netvigator.com 🚇 Central ⏰ 10am-7pm ⑤ free

Shanghai Street Artspace Exhibition Hall (2, B2)

Funded by the Hong Kong Arts Development Council, this small space in a strange location concentrates on new art by local artists. Video assemblages, photography, computer art and mixed media all get a look-in. ✉ 404 Shanghai St, Yau Ma Tei ☎ 2770 2157 🚇 Yau Ma Tei ⏰ 10.30am-7.30pm (closed Wed) ⑤ free

MARKETS

Cat St Market (4, C2)

Lascar Row is the official name of this pedestrian-only laneway lined with antique and curio shops and stalls selling found objects, cheap jewellery, ornaments, carvings and newly minted ancient coins. Cat St is a fun place to prowl around for a trinket or two.

✉ **Lascar Row (off Ladder St), Sheung Wan**
🚇 Sheung Wan
🕐 noon-10pm

Find charming charms at Sheung Wan.

Jade Jinx

The Chinese attribute various spiritual qualities to jade, including the power to prevent ageing and to deter evil spirits. Legend deems it bad luck for a jade merchant to say *chaoleng-fan* ('leftover fried rice') because the same expression describes a badly made jade object.

Sea of green gems

Jade Market (3, B3)

This market comprises a couple of hundred stalls selling all varieties and grades of jade from inside a large tent. Unless you really know your jade, it's probably not wise to buy any expensive pieces here.

✉ **Kansu St near**

Gascoigne Rd overpass, just west of Nathan Rd, Yau Ma Tei 🚇 Jordan/ Yau Ma Tei 🚌 9
🕐 10am-3.30pm

Li Yuen St (6, B5)

Actually two streets, Li Yuen St East and Li Yuen St West run parallel to each other between Des Voeux and Queen's Rds, opposite the Lane Crawford department store. Closed to motorised traffic, the lanes are crammed with shops selling clothing, fabrics and assorted knick-knacks.

✉ **Li Yuen Sts East & West, Central**
🚇 Central

Stanley Market (2, E4)

No big bargains, no big stings, just reasonably priced casual clothes, knick knacks, toys and formulaic art, all in a nicely confusing maze of alleys near the foreshore. It's not worth a trip in itself but combined with a meal and a wander around Stanley, the market can seem almost magical.

🚌 6, 6a, 6x or 260x (from Exchange Sq)
🕐 Mon-Fri 10am-5.30pm, Sat-Sun 10am-7pm 💲 free

Tung Choi St (Ladies') Market (2, B2)

The Tung Choi St market, two blocks east of Mong Kok MTR station (see p. 48), mainly sells cheap clothes. People start setting up their stalls as early as noon, but it's better to get here between 6-10pm, when there's much more on offer.

✉ **Tung Choi St (btw Nelson & Shantung Sts), Mong Kok**
🚇 Mong Kok
🕐 6pm-midnight

Western Market

(4, B2) Opposite the Macau ferry terminal, this 4-storey Edwardian building, built in 1906, was reopened in 1991 as a shopping centre. It's filled with modern shops selling all kinds of small antiques, collectibles and embroideries. The 1st floor is a 'cloth alley', similar to the fast-disappearing outdoor markets. Some good silks can be bought here.

✉ **Connaught Rd West (cnr Chung Kong Rd), Sheung Wan**
🚇 Sheung Wan
🕐 10am-7pm

PARKS, GARDENS & PUBLIC SPACES

Hong Kong Zoological & Botanic Gardens (4, G5)

These excellent gardens, established in 1864, are a pleasant collection of fountains, sculptures, greenhouses, aviaries, a zoo and a playground. There are hundreds of species of birds, exotic trees, plants and shrubs on display. The animal displays seem to be mostly primates; other residents include a lone jaguar. Don't come if you find small concrete cages upsetting. The gardens are divided by Albany Rd, with the plants and aviaries in one area, off Garden Rd, and most of the animals in the other.

There are people too at the zoo.

✉ Garden Rd, Central
☎ 2530 0154
🚇 Central 🚌 3, 12
⏰ 6am-10pm (zoo open till 7pm, greenhouse 9am-4.30pm)
⑤ free ♿ yes

Kowloon City Walled Park (2, A3)

The walls that enclose this beautiful park were once the perimeter of a notorious village which technically remained part of China throughout British rule. The enclave was known for its vice, prostitution, gambling and illegal dentists. In 1984 the Hong Kong government acquired the area, evicted the residents and replaced them with pavilions, ponds, turtles, goldfish and exquisite flora, including a long hedge coaxed into the form of a dragon. The park opened in 1996.

✉ Cnr Tung Tau Tsuen & Tung Tsing Rds, Kowloon City 🚇 Lok Fu (then taxi or 15mins walk along Junction Rd & Tung Tau Tsuen Rd)
🚌 1 (from Mong Kok MTR or Star Ferry)
⏰ 6.30am-11pm
⑤ free ♿ ramps, toilets

Kowloon Park (3, F3)

Once the site of the Whitfield Barracks for British and Indian troops, this area has been reborn as an oasis of green and a refreshing escape from the clutter and bustle of Nathan Rd. Pathways and walls crisscross the grass, birds hop around in cages, and towers and viewpoints dot the landscape. The Sculpture Walk features works by local artists. There's an excellent indoor/outdoor pool complex complete with waterfalls. If you wish to swim, go on a weekday morning or afternoon; on weekends there are so many bathers it's tough to even see the water.

✉ Bounded by Nathan, Canton, Austin & Haiphong Rds, Tsim Sha Tsui ☎ 2724 4100
🚇 Tsim Sha Tsui/Jordan
⏰ 6am-midnight (pools: Apr-Oct) ⑤ free

Maid in Hong Kong

On Sundays, Hong Kong's Filipino maids take over the pavements and public squares of Central. They come in their hundreds to share food, gossip, play cards and do one another's hair. You can't miss them around Statue Sq, Exchange Sq and the Hongkong & Shanghai Bank. There are about 140,000 Filipino maids in Hong Kong, most of them on two-year visas.

Statue Square

(4, E6) Statue Square once displayed effigies of England's royalty. The statues were taken down by the Japanese during WWII. Fittingly the sole survivor is a bronze likeness of Sir Thomas Jackson, a particularly successful Victorian-era head of the Hongkong & Shanghai Bank. On the north side of Chater Rd is the cenotaph dedicated to Hong Kong residents who died in both world wars. The ornate colonial building on the east side of the square is the former Supreme Court, which now serves as the Legislative Council Chamber.

✉ **Chater Rd, Central**
🚇 **Central**
⛴ **Star Ferry**

Tsim Sha Tsui Promenade (3, K3)

Along with Victoria Peak, this waterfront walkway offers some of the best views in Hong Kong. It's a lovely place to stroll during the day, and at night the views are mesmerising. You can walk along the water from the Star Ferry terminal all the way to the Hong Kong Coliseum and Kowloon KCR terminus. Midway along the promenade is a ferry pier where you can catch a hoverferry to HK Island. The promenade becomes a sea of people during the Chinese New Year fireworks display and again during the mid-summer Dragon Boat Festival.

✉ **Parallels Salisbury Rd along Victoria Harbour, Tsim Sha Tsui East** 🚇 **Tsim Sha Tsui** ⛴ **Star Ferry/HKF Hoverferry**

Victoria Park (5, E4)

One of the biggest patches of green grass on the northern side of HK Island, Victoria Park is also one of the territory's most popular escapes. The best time to stroll around is daytime during the week. Early in the morning this is an excellent place to watch the slow-motion choreography of practitioners of taijiquan. The evening is given over to Hong Kong's young lovers. Between April and October you can take a dip in the swimming pool. The park becomes a flower market a few days before the Chinese New Year. It's also worth a visit during the Mid-Autumn (Moon) Festival.

✉ **East of Causeway Bay** 🚇 **Causeway Bay**

Yuen Po St Bird Garden (2, B2)

There are hundreds of birds for sale here along with elaborate cages carved from teak and bamboo. The Chinese have long favoured birds as pets, especially those that can sing. The singing prowess of a bird often determines its price. Some birds are also considered harbingers of good fortune, which is why they are sometimes

Behind Bars

The bamboo cages you see at the bird market are intricately crafted. The best cages are repeatedly soaked, softened and dried as they are shaped, sometimes up to 10 times.

Going for a song

taken to horse races. The birds seem to live pretty well: the Chinese use chopsticks to feed live grasshoppers to their feathered friends, and give them honey nectar to gild their vocal cords.

✉ **Boundary St (behind Mong Kok Stadium), Yau Ma Tei (see p. 48)** 🚇 **Prince Edward** 🚌 **1, 1a** 🚉 **Mong Kok KCR** 🕐 **8am-7pm** 💲 **free** ♿ **accessible toilets**

Ambulate with view along Tsim Sha Tsui.

QUIRKY HONG KONG

Sure, we've all strapped a kid to a bamboo pole and waved him or her around in a parade. Who of us hasn't made a half-coffee/half-tea cuppa, just for kicks? And of course we all throw oranges high into a tree when we want to give fate a hop along. We just don't do them all on the same day, which is what you can do in Hong Kong.

Central Market

(6, A4) You shouldn't have any trouble finding this huge wholesale market – just sniff the air. It's more a zoo than a market, with everything from chickens and quail to eels and crabs, alive or freshly slaughtered. The squeamish should give it a miss.

✉ Btw Des Voeux & Queen's Rds and Jubilee & Queen Victoria Sts, Central
☎ 2869 8802
🚇 Central 🚢 Star Ferry ⏰ 5am-noon

Act Normal, Do Strange

If you want to have a day you can *really* tell your friends about, do like this:

- breakfast on pig organ congee at Happy Garden (p. 79)
- buy some party-bondage gear at Onitsuka (p. 57)
- walk over the Longevity Bridge at Repulse Bay (p. 27)
- have a *yuan yang* (half-coffee/half-tea) at Dai Pai Dong (p. 70)
- read out some of your best poetry at Visage Free (p. 94)

Central-Mid-Levels Escalator (6, A4-E1)

The 'world's longest covered outdoor people mover' is part commuter travelator, part sightseeing ride and part pick-up procession. It consists of elevated escalators, moving walkways and linking stairs which cover the 800m hill from Central's offices to the Mid-Levels' apartments. The funniest bit is past the Shelley St bars – travelators have just enough time to flirt with barflies as they glide by.

✉ Cochrane, Shelley & Peel Sts, Central/Mid-Levels 🚇 Central
⏰ Downhill 6-10am; uphill 10.20am-midnight 💲 free

Cheung Chau Bun Festival (1, G4)

The Bun Festival of Tai Chiu takes place in May and is famous for its bun towers – bamboo scaffolding standing up to 20m high and covered with holy bread buns. On the 3rd day of the festival (a Sunday) there's a lively procession with stilt walkers and colourfully dressed 'floating children' who are carried through the streets strapped to long waving poles.

✉ Pak Tai Temple, Pak She St, Cheung Chau
🚢 Cheung Chau (from Central)
💲 free

Noonday Gun (5, E3)

One of the few vestiges of Causeway Bay's colonial past is this recoil-mounted, 3lb cannon built by Hotchkiss in Portsmouth in 1901. It stands in front of the Excelsior Hotel, accessible via a tunnel under the road from the World Trade Centre, and is fired daily at noon. Exactly how this tradition started is not known. Noel Coward made the gun famous with his satirical 1924 song 'Mad Dogs and Englishmen', about colonists who braved the heat of the noonday sun while the locals stayed indoors: *'In Hong Kong they strike a gong/and fire off a noonday gun/to reprimand each inmate/who's in late.'*

✉ 281 Gloucester Rd, Causeway Bay
🚇 Causeway Bay

Wishing Tree (1, C6)

If you're crossing your fingers and avoiding the cracks but still haven't got lucky, pay a visit to the wishing tree. This large banyan beauty is laden with wishes written on swatches of paper tied to an orange. You write your wish on the fruit and then throw it as high as you can into the tree. The higher it goes, the more chance there is of your wish coming true.

✉ Lam Tsuen, Lam Kam Rd, Tai Po 🚉 Tai Po KCR (then bus 64k)
💲 free

KEEPING FIT

Walking and taijiquan are the most popular physical activities undertaken locally. Golf is a rich person's sport, undertaken more for its networking possibilities and prestige than its physical benefits. Tennis is quite popular and gyms have caught on with the younger generation. All top-end hotels have gyms and most have swimming pools. Kowloon Park (see p. 42) has a public swimming pool that's more leisure pool than a place for serious lappers.

Discovery Bay Golf Club (1, E4)
This 18-hole course is open to visitors Monday, Tuesday & Friday but you need to book two days in advance. ✉ Discovery Bay, Lantau ☎ 2987 7273; bookings ☎ 2987 2112 🚢 Star Ferry (from Central) ⑤ green fees $1400

Lamma Yoga Centre (2, D1)
Satyananda yoga and meditation classes in a hippy scene. The Bookworm Cafe is a great post-yoga hang-out for cups of tea and sustenance. ✉ 59 Back St, Yung Shue Wan (behind Bookworm Cafe), Lamma ☎ 2982 0270 🚢 Yung Shue Wan (from Central) ⊙ Mon, Tues & Thurs evening, Sat morning ⑤ $120/class

New York's fit staff

New York Fitness Gym (6, C3)
This well-equipped gym has free weights, resistance training, punch bags and all manner of fitness class. It's right by the Central-Mid-Levels escalator so you can impress passing trade while pumping the cycle machine. ✉ 32 Hollywood Rd, Soho ☎ 2543 2280 🚇 Central ↘ ⊙ Mon-Fri 6.45am-10.30pm, Sat-Sun 7.30am-9pm ⑤ $500/week

Paradise Ladies Health Club (4, G11)
This gym might suit women who would rather work up a sweat without male company. Also has facials and other beauty treatments. ✉ 20th fl, 23 Thomson Rd, Wan Chai ☎ 2529 5252 🚇 Wan Chai ⊙ Mon-Fri 7.30am-10pm, Sat-Sun noon-6pm ⑤ monthly memberships; call for prices

Taijiquan Lessons (4, G7)
The HKTA offers beginner taijiquan classes for tourists. The slow, graceful exercises have a meditative quality and help balance, muscle tone and digestion. Wear comfy clothes and sports shoes to these one-hour classes. ✉ Garden Plaza, Hong Kong Park, Admiralty ☎ 2508 1234 🚇 Admiralty ⊙ Tues, Fri & Sun 8.15am ⑤ free

Victoria Park Tennis Centre (5, D5)
There are 13 tennis courts at this easy-to-find complex near Tin Hau station. You're more likely to snare a court if you can play during business hours. ✉ Hing Fat St, Victoria Park, Causeway Bay ☎ 2570 6186 🚇 Tin Hau ⊙ 6am-11pm ⑤ day: $42/hr, evening: $57/hr

Yoga Central (6, D5)
Hatha Yoga with an Iyengar spin. Beginner and intermediate classes Mon-Sat; ring ahead to reserve. ✉ 4th fl, 13 Wyndham St, Lan Kwai Fong ☎ 2982 4308 🚇 Central ⑤ hour-long class $120

Just Reward

If your travel-weary muscles scream *massage*, try the following:

Healing Plants (6, C4; ☎ 2815 5005, healguru@netvigator.com), 17 Lyndhurst Tce, Central – acupuncture, reflexology, Swedish massage and other therapies

New Paradise Health Club (5, F1; ☎ 2574 8916), 414 Lockhart Rd, Wan Chai – traditional Chinese massage, sauna, steam bath, pedicure and manicure

out & about

WALKING TOURS
Central Amble

Begin at the Star Ferry pier **(1)** in Central. With your back to the water, take the elevated walkway to the right and follow signs to Exchange Square **(2)** and Jardine House **(3)**. Using the walkway, cross over to the south side of Connaught Rd. Turn left past the Mandarin Oriental Hotel to Statue Square **(4)**. Head left along Chater Rd, turn right at Murray Rd and follow signs for the pedestrian walkway to the Bank of China tower **(5)**. Retrace your steps then veer right, past the Flagstaff House Museum **(6)** in Hong Kong Park **(7)**. Walkways west across Cotton Tree Dr and Garden Rd drop you off at St John's Cathedral **(8)**. Take

distance 2km **duration** 1hr
start 🚢 Star Ferry 🚇 Central
end 🚇 Central

Join Central's hustlers and bustlers.

Battery Path down to Queen's Rd at the corner of Ice House St. There's an entrance to the classy Landmark **(9)** shopping centre here – Fountainside is one of many good eateries inside. Back on Queen's Rd, the Hongkong & Shanghai Bank **(10)** is one block to the east. Walk through the ground floor plaza: entrance K to Central Station is accessible from the western side of Statue Square.

Sheung Wan Shuffle

Browse Des Voeux Rd West's dried seafood shops **(1)** then turn up Ko Shing St where there are traditional herbal wholesalers **(2)**. At the end of the street, walk briefly along Des Voeux Rd and turn right onto Bonham Strand West, which is lined with wholesale ginseng sellers **(3)**. Hook right onto Bonham Strand and up to Queen's Rd West. To the left you'll find shops selling bird's nests (for soup!) and paper funeral offerings for the dead **(4)**. Across Queen's Rd is Possession St **(5)**, where Captain Charles Elliot first planted the Union Jack in 1841. Climbing Pound Lane to where it meets Tai Ping Shan St, look to the right to find the Pak Sing Temple **(6)**, built in the 1850s to hold ancestral tablets brought over from China. Descend Upper Station St to Hollywood Rd's antique shops **(7)**. Continuing east on Hollywood Rd will bring you to Man Mo Temple **(8)**. Take a short hop down Ladder St to Upper Lascar Row, home of Cat St market **(9)**. Ladder St will bring you to Queen's Rd again, which you can cross to Hillier St **(10)** for a street stall snack. On Bonham Strand, head east to find Man Wa Lane **(11)** where you can have a traditional chop, or seal, made.

SIGHTS & HIGHLIGHTS
dried seafood shops
herbal wholesalers and ginseng sellers
bird's nests
Possession St
Pak Sing Temple
antique shops (p. 65)
Man Mo Temple (p. 23)
Cat St market (p. 41)
street stalls
Man Wa Lane

Aphrodisiacs 'R' Us – Chinese medicine shops have a cure for most ills.

distance 1.9km **duration** 1hr
start Kennedy Town to Sutherland St
end Sheung Wan

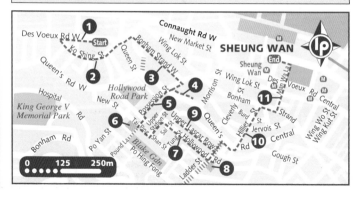

Mong Kok to Jordan Mooch

Take exit A from Prince Edward MTR, walk north up Nathan Rd, then turn right onto Boundary St. The Yuen Po St Bird Garden **(1)** is 10mins walk away. Continue out the back to Flower Market Rd **(2)** where there are lovely blooms to behold. At the end of the street, turn left onto Sai Yee St, then right onto Prince Edward Rd West. At Tung Choi St turn left: the first couple of blocks are dominated by goldfish shops **(3)**. South of Argyle Rd, the Ladies' Market **(4)** takes over. Turn right at Dundas St – Trendy Zone **(5)** is on the corner of Nathan Rd. Cross over and turn left into Shanghai St where there's an art gallery **(6)** at No 404 and a woodcarving shop at No 342. Cut down Hi Lung Lane to Temple St where you can snack at Hing Kee

Fans of feathered friends flock to Yuen Po Bird Garden.

distance 4.5km **duration** 2hrs
start Ⓜ Prince Edward
end Ⓜ Jordan

(7). The night market **(8)** runs on both sides of Public Square St, separated by Tin Hau Temple **(9)** and the Jade Market **(10)**. If you want to rest, see what's showing at Broadway Cinematheque **(11)**; there's a cafe here too.

Night Light

Festive they may be, but those pink and green neon arrows strung along Mong Kok's streets are code for brothels. You'll also see a lot of 'hourly' hotels. Though Mong Kok is a pretty seedy part of town, there's no appreciable rise in street crime to go along with it.

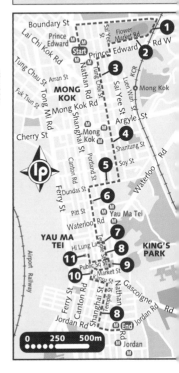

Cheung Chau Canter

Disembark the ferry and turn left past Praya St's restaurants into Pak She Praya Rd, from where you'll see houseboats in the harbour. Take Pak She Fourth Lane to Pak Tai Temple **(1)**, site of the Bun Festival. Head south along Pak She St and dogleg into San Hing St past traditional shops selling paper offerings, herbs and incense. Turn left at Tung Wan Rd – the Garden Café **(2)** at No 84 has good Western food. The beach **(3)** at the end of the street is popular with windsurfers and swimmers. Walk south along the shore, behind the Warwick Hotel **(4)**, onto Cheung Chau Sports Rd, then right onto Kwun Yum Wan Rd. You'll soon come to the Kwan Kung Pavilion **(5)**, dedicated to Kwan Tai, the God of War and Righteousness. A left turn out of the temple will put you on Peak Rd which leads along a scenic ridge, past a cemetery (take the right fork) down to the ferry pier at Sai Wan **(6)**. It's especially lovely at dusk. Either take a boat back to Cheung Chau village (where you began) or take the path to Cheung Po Tsai Cave **(7)**, an old pirate hang-out. Back at Cheung Chau village, round off your day with some fresh seafood on the waterfront.

SIGHTS & HIGHLIGHTS

Pak Tai Temple (see Bun Festival, p. 44)
Garden Café
Tung Wan Beach
Warwick Hotel
Kwan Kung Pavilion
Sai Wan
Cheung Po Tsai Cave

Hong Kong Tourist Association

Kids fly high during May's Bun Festival.

distance 4.5km **duration** 2.5hrs
start Central-Cheung Chau
end Cheung Chau-Central

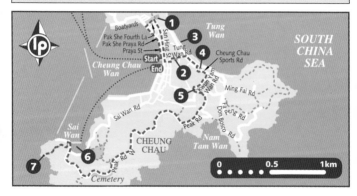

EXCURSIONS
Lamma (2, E1)

The third-largest island, after Lantau and Hong Kong, Lamma is *the* haven for expats. Known mainly for its seafood restaurants, Lamma also has good beaches and hikes.

Walking between the two main townships, **Yung Shue Wan** and **Sok Kwu Wan**, takes just over an hour via popular **Hung Shing Ye beach**. South of the beach, the path

Lamma to Aberdeen Loop

You can make a nice round trip by catching the ferry to Yung Shue Wan, walking across the island to Sok Kwu Wan and then catching the ferry to Aberdeen. As you enter Aberdeen Harbour, you'll see as much boat life as you would on a sampan ride (p. 53). Your hardest decision: to sup a seafood meal at Sok Kwu Wan or wait for the Jumbo Floating Restaurant (p. 77).

INFORMATION

10km south of Central

🚢 Central/Aberdeen-Yung Shue Wan/Sok Kwu Wan

ⓘ Hong Kong & Kowloon Ferry ☎ 2815 6063

💲 Yung Shue Wan/Sok Kwu Wan to: Central ($10-20); Aberdeen ($7-12)

✗ Bookworm Café, Yung Shue Wan Main St (organic); Tai Yuen, 15 First St, Sok Kwu Wan (seafood)

Lamma Lookout

climbs steeply until it reaches a pavilion near the top of the hill. This is a nice place to relax, despite the clear view of the power station. You soon come to a ridge where you can look down on Sok Kwu Wan, a small place supporting a dozen or more fine waterfront seafood restaurants.

Lantau (1, G2)

Lantau is 142 sq km, almost twice the size of Hong Kong Island. More than half of this sparsely populated mountainous island has been declared country parks.

There are good hikes, interesting villages and monasteries, including the Buddhist **Po Lin Monastery**. On a hill above the monastery is the **Tiantan Buddha Statue**, a 22m bronze beauty.

The 70km-long Lantau Trail loops around the island from Mui Wo. The middle section of the trail (the most scenic part) is accessible from Po Lin at Ngong Ping. It's 17.5km (or 7hrs) from Ngong Ping to Mui Wo, via Lantau and

INFORMATION

20-30km west of Central

🚇 Tung Chung/Airport

🚢 Central/Tsim Sha Tsui-Mui Wo then bus No 2 to Po Lin; Star Ferry-Discovery Bay

ⓘ First Ferry Co ☎ 2131 8181; CPA (parks info) ☎ 2422 9431
   📧 www.afdparks.gov.hk

💲 ferry $15-31

✗ *The Stoep*, 32 Lwr Cheung Sha Village (Sth African on the beach)

The titanic Tiantan Buddha

Sunset Peak. The airport adjoins Lantau so you can work in a trip to the island's attractions with your arrival or departure from Hong Kong.

Sai Kung   (1, D8)

The Sai Kung Peninsula is the last chunk of Hong Kong, apart from the outlying islands, that remains a haven for hikers, swimmers and boating enthusiasts. Decades ago, pirates and tigers roamed the peninsula. These days, the occasional stray dogs might be a walkers only worry. Sai Kung town is an excellent point from which to hike into the surrounding region and then return for delicious seafood on the waterfront in the evening.

INFORMATION

25km northeast of Central

🚌 Choi Hung MTR then Public Light bus 1 (20mins), or bus 92 (30mins) to Sai Kung town. Bus 94 goes to the Maclehose Trail.

ⓘ CPA ☎ 2422 9431
    🇪 www.afdparks.gov.hk

🕐 Visitor Centre Wed-Mon 9.30am-4.30pm

🍴 Chuen Kee (p. 76)

A short journey to one of the islands off Sai Kung town is rewarding. Hidden away are some excellent beaches that are worth visiting on a *kaido* (small boat). Kaidos leave from the waterfront in Sai Kung town. Most head over to **Sharp Island** (Kiu Tsui Chau) about 1.5km away. Hap Mun Bay, a sandy beach in the south of the island, is served as is Kiu Tsui Bay to the west.

The **Maclehose Trail**, a 100km route across the New Territories, begins near Sai Kung. The first few km of the trail around Hoi Ha Wan reveal fantastic coastal scenery. There's a wheelchair accessible picnic area just near the visitor centre at Pak Tam Chung.

Shek O   (2, D5)

Shek O has one of the best beaches on Hong Kong Island. The village is small, so it's easy to get your bearings. Between the bus stop and the beach you'll pass some restaurants; if you take the road leading off to the left you'll enter a maze of small homes, which grow in size and luxury as you head along the peninsula. This is the **Shek O headlands**, home to some of Hong Kong's wealthiest families. At the tip of the peninsula there's a look out over the South China Sea: next stop, the Philippines.

You can also approach Shek O by foot, along the spectacular **Dragon's Back Trail**. This final 4km of the 50km Hong Kong Trail takes about 2.5hrs, finishing at Big Wave Bay, 2km north of Shek O. You can have a cooling dip here or walk on to Shek O.

INFORMATION

10km south of Central

🚌 Shau Kei Wan MTR then bus 9 to Shek O or bus 14 to To Te Wan to walk the Dragon's Back Trail

ⓘ CPA ☎ 2422 9431
    🇪 www.afdparks.gov.hk

🍴 Welcome Garden (p. 78)

Colin K Barnes

Take a flying leap at Shek O.

Stanley (2, E4)

About 2000 people lived at Stanley when the British took over in 1841, making it one of the island's largest settlements at the time. The British built a prison near the village in 1937 – just in time to be used by the Japanese to intern the expatriates. Now it's used as a maximum security prison.

The main attraction is **Stanley Market** (p. 41) and the local restaurants; there's an OK beach where you can rent windsurfers. At the western end of the bay is **Murray House** moved brick by brick from the current Bank of China site and newly opened as an upscale cafe and shop. Visit Stanley during the week: it's bursting with tourists and locals on weekends.

INFORMATION

15km south of Central
🚌 6, 6a, 6x, 260x (from Exchange Sq)
🍴 Lucy's (p. 77)

Artists ply their trade at Stanley Market.

Macau (7, E1)

Only 90mins ferry ride from Hong Kong, this Latin-Asian fusion makes a great getaway. A Portuguese colony until 1999, Macau is now a special administrative region of China. This tiny (23.5 sq km) SAR is divided into the Macau Peninsula, which is attached to China, and the two islands of Taipa and Coloane, connected by bridges. About 95% of the population is Chinese and most tourists are Chinese gamblers drawn to the casinos.

INFORMATION

65km west of Central
🚢 from HK Island or Kowloon China Ferry terminal (see p. 107)
ⓘ Macau Gov Tourist Office, 9 Large do Senado, Macau ☎ 853-315 566
📧 www.macautourism.gov.mo
💲 ferry $90-150
🍴 Bolo de Arroz, 11 Travessa de Santo Domingos (cafe); Fernando's, 9 Praia de Hac Sa (seafood & beer)

The following attractions could easily be seen in one day. The marvellous **Ruinas de São Paulo** (Ruins of St Paul's Cathedral), at the end of Rua da São Paulo, were designed by an Italian Jesuit and built by Japanese Christian exiles in the early 1600s. All that remains today is the facade, the mosaic floor and the stone steps.

The peaceful, verdant **Lou Lim Ioc Gardens**, on Avenida do Conselheiro Ferreira de Almeida, sport a mixture of 'European and Chinese plants, with huge shady trees, lotus ponds, pavilions, bamboo groves and grottoes. The **Maritime Museum**, Rua do São Tiago da Barra, houses a world-class collection related to Macau's seafaring past. There's a flower boat, a tugboat, a Chinese fishing vessel, and a dragon boat that is used in races during the Dragon Boat Festival. To round off your day, catch a bus to Coloane's **Hac Sa Beach** for a swim and a meal.

ORGANISED TOURS

Tourism is one of Hong Kong's main money earners, so it's no surprise that there is a mind-boggling number of tours available. Some of the best tours are offered by the HKTA. As well as the standard major sight excursions, they run harbour cruises, island boat trips and day trips to the New Territories. They also have a series of thematic tours covering subjects such as horse racing, folk customs and healthy living, Chinese style. During the March food festival, there are tasting tours to restaurants and homes. Call the special tour line on ☎ 2807 6390 or drop in to an HKTA office.

Bus Tours Dozens of operators offer sightseeing tours around Hong Kong, Kowloon and the New Territories. If you only have a short time in Hong Kong, or are not in the mood to deal with public transport and taxi drivers, these may be just what you need. Most tour operators do hotel pick-ups.

Boat Trips As well as getting Hong Kong's best views, a trip on the water means you can visit some of the outlying islands. Many tours combine a cruise past the Hong Kong Island skyline with a visit to fishing villages or beaches that you might not find on your own.

Walking Tours The HKTA produces some good self-guided audio tours of architecture and monuments throughout Hong Kong. Guided bushwalking tours are available in many country parks. There's even a tour which explains the fung shui of Hong Kong's skyscrapers!

Night Tours Most boat tour operators run some trips after dark when the Hong Kong lights are twinkling and you can't see how filthy the water is. Evening bus tours take in restaurants and a tame version of the nightlife.

Sampan Surfing

Fishing is banned in the South China Sea during July and August so most of Aberdeen's fishing fleet is in the harbour over summer. It's the best time to take a sampan ride – you'll see people sprucing up their boats, mending nets and going about daily houseboat life.

Tours can be arranged at the Aberdeen Promenade. If you are by yourself, hang out by the harbour and wait for the old women who operate the boats to invite you to join a tour.

Eric L Wheater

Sampan and junk jam, Aberdeen

Aberdeen & Harbour Night Cruise (4, D4)

A spin around the harbour which includes a seafood dinner at a fishing village en route.

✉ **HKTA, The Center, 99 Queen's Rd Central, Central** ☎ **2807 6390** ⑤ **$680/$540** ⊘ **nightly**

Come Horseracing

(4, D4) The HKTA operates tours to race meetings at Happy Valley, Hong Kong Island and Sha Tin, New Territories. Tours include coach transfers from hotels on both sides of the harbour. The tour is not available to children; you must wear smart clothing.

✉ **HKTA, Central (see above)** ⑤ **EZ Race $120; Classic Tour $490** ⊘ **pick-ups from Wed 5.45pm & Sat 11.15am**

Pretty in pink dolphins

Hong Kong Tourist Association

Dolphinwatch

(3, J3) As well as a scenic dolphin-spotting expedition, this 4hr tour raises environmental awareness. Up to 160 pink dolphins live in the Hong Kong's dirty, bustling waters.

✉ **1528a Star House, Salisbury Rd, Tsim Sha Tsui** ☎ **2984 1414** ⑤ **$280/$140** ⊘ **Wed, Fri, Sat 8.30am-1pm (call for expanded schedule)**

Gray Line (3, G5)

This stalwart tour company has a variety of tours. 'Highlight of the Night' involves happy hour on the harbour, dinner at a revolving restaurant and a visit to nightspots in Wan Chai and Lan Kwai Fong.

✉ **5th fl, Cheong Hing Bldg, 72 Nathan Rd, Tsim Sha Tsui** ☎ **2368 7111** ⑤ **$610/$510** ⊘ **nightly**

Heritage & Architecture Walks (4, D4)

Audio equipment for self-guided walking tours around Hong Kong, Kowloon and the New Territories. Pick gear up from HKTA offices in The Center and the Star Ferry terminal, Tsim Sha Tsui.

✉ **HKTA, Central (see above)** ☎ **2508 1234** ⑤ **$50 (plus $500 refundable deposit)**

Kaarlo Schepel

(5, E3) HKTA-approved Kaarlo Schepel leads small groups on hikes through Kowloon and the New Territories' forested areas.

✉ **meet: Excelsior Hotel, 281 Gloucester Rd, Causeway Bay** ☎ **2577 6319** ⑤ **$275** ⊘ **Kowloon: Mon, Fri 9am; New Territories: Thurs 9am**

The Land Between

(4, D4) This 6hr New Territories tour takes you to places that it would be a hassle to get to yourself. Tai Mo Shan (Hong Kong's highest peak) and a village near the mainland border are included.

✉ **HKTA, Central (see above)** ☎ **2807 6390** ⑤ **$385/$335** ⊘ **pick-ups daily from 8.30am**

Lantau Tours (1, F4)

Two different day-long itineraries are offered: one visits Lantau's beaches and fishing villages, the other stops at the Tsing Ma Bridge. Both pay a visit to the Tiantan Buddha statue.

✉ **Shop E, Silver Centre, Silvermine Bay, Lantau** ☎ **2984 8255** ⑤ **$550/$380** ⊘ **daily**

Sky Bird Travel Agency

(3, F5) An architecture walk with a difference, this fung shui tour points out the harmonies – and disharmonies – of some of the city's famous skyscrapers.

✉ **Room 803, Koon Fook Centre, 9 Knutsford Tce, Tsim Sha Tsui** ☎ **2369 9628** ⑤ **$280/$240** ⊘ **Tues, Fri**

Splendid Tours & Travel

(3, H4) A variety of packages including a 'sea and land tour' which crams Hong Kong's major sights into one day. Also ask about guided tours to China, both day and overnight.

✉ **26th fl, 25-27 Lock Rd, Tsim Sha Tsui** ☎ **2316 2151** ⑤ **$480 ($390 children)** ⊘ **daily**

Star Cruises (3, H3)

If you want an easy weekend out of Honkers, a short cruise on the *SuperStar Leo* might be just the ticket. There are restaurants, a nightclub and all sorts of leisure facilities aboard.

✉ **1501 Ocean Centre, Tsim Sha Tsui** ☎ **2317 7711** ⑤ **various** ⊘ **departures weekly**

shopping

Shopping in Hong Kong goes way beyond buying stuff you need: it's a social activity, a favourite recreation, an after-hours release. And though it isn't the bargain basement it once was, Honkers still wins for variety and its passionate embrace of competitive consumerism. Any international brand worthy of its own perfume sets up shop here, and there are a slew of local brands worth your money too. Clothing, jewellery and electronics are the city's strong suits – all of them can be made to order whether it's an Armani-copy ensemble, a pair of earrings or a PC.

Shopping Areas

The main shopping areas are Tsim Sha Tsui, Central and Causeway Bay. **Nathan Rd**, Tsim Sha Tsui, is the main tourist strip, and the only place where you'll find spruikers. It's also the place you're most likely to get ripped off, especially on electronics or cameras. **Central** has a mix of mid-range to top-end shopping centres and street-front retail; it's popular with locals and tourists. This is a good area to look for cameras, books, antiques and designer threads. **Causeway Bay** is a crush of department stores and smaller outlets selling eclectic fashion. It's a madhouse on weekends. For market shopping, see p. 41.

Opening Hours

You can more or less expect shops to be open 10am to 6pm daily. In Causeway Bay and Wan Chai, many will stay open until 9.30pm. In Tsim Sha Tsui and Yau Ma Tei, shops close around 9pm. If shops take a day off, it's usually Monday; they may also be closed Sunday morning.

Smart Buying

Most shops are loathe to give refunds but they can usually be persuaded to exchange untampered purchases: make sure you get a detailed receipt which enumerates the goods as well as the payment. When buying electronics, always beware of goods imported by a nonauthorised agent as this may void your warranty. If you have trouble with dodgy merchants in Hong Kong, call the Consumer Council on ☎ 2929 2222.

Strike a pose at Lane Crawford.

Paying & Bargaining

There are no sales taxes so the marked price is the price you'll pay. Credit cards are widely accepted, except in markets. It's rare for traders to accept travellers cheques or foreign currency as payment. Sales assistants in department or chain stores rarely have any leeway to give discounts but you can try bargaining in owner-operated stores and certainly in markets. If you've loaded up big, stores will usually be happy to ship items home for you.

DEPARTMENT STORES

Lane Crawford
(6, B5) The original branch of Hong Kong's first western-style department store. It's still an upscale place but doesn't have the prestige of the early days. Other branches in Admiralty (Pacific Place) and Causeway Bay (Times Square).
✉ **70 Queen's Rd, Central** ☎ **2524 7875**
Ⓔ **Central**
🕐 **10am-7.30pm**

Marks & Spencer
(3, H3) Britain's well-known chain is a good

On your mark...

place for undies, simple coordinates, sensible shoes and accessories like sun-hats and brollies. There's a scattering of branches including in Admiralty (Pacific Place), Causeway Bay (Pearl City Plaza, 22 Paterson St and Times Square) and Central (28 Queen's Rd).
✉ **Ocean Centre, Harbour City, 5 Canton Rd, Tsim Sha Tsui**
☎ **2926 3330** Ⓔ **Tsim Sha Tsui** 🕐 **10am-7pm**

Sogo (5, F3)
This Japanese-owned store is the hub of Causeway Bay with 12 well-organised floors. The range is mind-boggling: over 20 brands of neckties for just for starters. Eclectic departments include the 'baby train models' area and a culture centre with patchwork and oil painting displays.
✉ **555 Hennessy Rd,**

Causeway Bay ☎ **2833 8338** Ⓔ **Causeway Bay** 🕐 **10am-10pm**

It's all gogo at Sogo.

Wing On (4, C3)
This Hong Kong department store has a branch in Central and a new one on Nathan Rd, Yau Ma Tei. Though it's notable for being locally owned, in the end it's nothing special. There's another location at 345 Nathan Rd, Jordan.
✉ **211 Des Voeux Rd, Central** ☎ **2524 7875**
Ⓔ **Central**
🕐 **10am-7.30pm**

Mall Trawl

Hong Kong is mall rat heaven but don't feel compelled to visit more than a couple: the same brands turn up over and over again. They include:

Harbour City (3, G2) Canton Rd, Tsim Sha Tsui – the biggest by far with 700 shops in four zones. Every major brand is represented in an overwhelming mix.

Pacific Place (4, G9) 88 Queensway, Admiralty – see p. 25.

Times Square (5, G2) 1 Matheson St, Causeway Bay – a dozen floors of retail organised by type. There's electronics (on 7th), a play area (on 9th) and food (on 12 & 13th).

International Finance Centre (IFC) Mall (4, D6) 1 Harbour View St, Central – a bright new centre with high-fashion boutiques, the great Eating Plus snackery and the Airport Express terminus downstairs. Toilets are in short supply.

The Landmark (4, E5) 1 Pedder St, Central – high fashion and good food in a pleasant open space. Many high-end international brands are represented.

Prince's Building (4, E6) 10 Chater Rd, Central – poky and disorienting but worth a look for its speciality fashion, toy and kitchenware shops. There are few toilets.

Festival Walk (2, A3) 80 Tat Chee Ave, Kowloon Tong – a new centre with a good middle-rung selection of shops, great disabled access and toilets on every level.

CLOTHING – WOMEN'S

Chau Ming Workshop (5, G2)
Knits and embroidered denims handmade in Hong Kong. Not exactly easy-to-wear (schlep through nearby Times Square for that) but definitely cute and one of a kind.
✉ Shop C, 11 Sharp St East, Causeway Bay
☎ 2891 8623
◉ Causeway Bay
🚌 5b ⏰ noon-10pm

Encyco (5, E3)
Independent young Hong Kong designer with an eye for wispy wear, verging on the wacky. One of many exciting couturiers in the Island Beverley enclave.
✉ Island Beverley, 1 Great George St, Causeway Bay ☎ 2504 1016 ◉ Causeway Bay
🚌 ⏰ Tues-Sun 2-9pm

Garex Ison (6, D5)
A local designer working with textures and layers to come up with stylish suits, tops and bottoms. One of a few frolicsome mid-market fashion outlets in this strip.
✉ 26 Wyndham St, Central ☎ 2537 3326
◉ Central 🚌 13, 26, 43 ⏰ Mon-Sat 11am-8pm

i.t (3, F3)
This shop and the b+ab store next door both sell the cute, trendy gear that surrounds on HK's streets. There are i.t and I.T stores in the major shopping areas (capitalisation denotes its 'grown up' range).
✉ Shop 1030, Miramar Centre, 1-23 Kimberley Rd, Tsim Sha Tsui
☎ 2736 9152 ◉ Tsim Sha Tsui ⏰ noon-10pm

Joyce Ma (4, F5)
This multi-designer store is a good choice if you're pressed for time: Issey Miyake, Yves Saint Laurent, Jean Paul Gaultier, Commes des Garçons, Voyage and Yohji Yamamoto are just some whose wearable wares are on display. Also at 334 Pacific Place, Admiralty and 23 Nathan Rd, Tsim Sha Tsui.
✉ New World Tower, 16 Queen's Rd Central, Central ☎ 2810 1120
◉ Central ⏰ Mon-Sat 10.30am-7.30pm, Sun noon-6pm

Miu Miu (4, E5)
Super-cute and creative threads for neo-adults ('oh they put a zip *there*'). The shoes are exceptionally stylish.
✉ Shop B24, The Landmark, 1 Pedder St, Central ☎ 2523 7833
◉ Central 🚢 Star Ferry ⏰ Mon-Sat 10am-7pm, Sun 11am-6pm

Onitsuka (3, E6)
Basic black threaded with trinkets, eyelets, studs and general naughtiness. Be made up, waxed, shaved

Onitsuka anyone?

and ready to party.
✉ 15c Austin Ave, Tsim Sha Tsui ☎ 2368 1085 ◉ Tsim Sha Tsui ⏰ Mon-Sat noon-9pm

Ozoc (4, E5)
Japanese designer gear for Chuppies (Chinese yuppies) who get into nifty girl-gear like lime-green dresses and plastic accessories.
✉ Shop B11, The Landmark, 1 Pedder St, Central ☎ 2234 9388
◉ Central ⏰ 10.30am-7.30pm

Pearls & Cashmere
(4, E6) Quality cuddly merchandise includes more cardigans than you want to see in a lifetime and a rainbow of pashmina, some of it deliciously embroidered.
✉ Shop M12, Mandarin Oriental Hotel, 5 Connaught Rd, Central ☎ 2525 6771
◉ Central 🚢 Star Ferry ⏰ Mon-Sat 9.30am-7pm, Sun 10am-5pm

Shanghai Tang
(4, E5) Started by flamboyant Hong Kong businessman David Tang, Shanghai Tang sparked something of a fashion wave in Hong Kong with its updated versions of traditional Chinese garments. Custom tailoring is available and they've expanded into accessories and gifts.
✉ Pedder Bldg, 12 Pedder St, Central
☎ 2525 7333
◉ Central 🚢 Star Ferry ⏰ Mon-Sat 10am-8pm, Sun noon-6pm (afternoon tea 3-6pm)

CLOTHING – MEN'S

Blanc De Chine (4, E5)
A sumptuous store specialising in traditional Chinese jackets, off the rack or made to measure. There's also a lovely selection of silk dresses (for women).
✉ Shop 201, Pedder Bldg, 12 Pedder St, Central ☎ 2524 7875 ⊕ Central ⚓ Star Ferry ⊘ Mon-Sat noon-7pm, Sun noon-5pm

Sew Sew

Most top hotels have tailors on-site: ask your concierge for advice. Otherwise, try **Pacific Custom Tailors** (4, G9; ☎ 2845 5377), Shop 322, Pacific Place, Admiralty, for men's and ladies' suits and shirts. The turnaround on most items is 48hrs including two fittings. Three top-quality shirts cost around $1100, men's suits range from $2500-5000. It's open Mon-Sat 9.30am-7pm.

Grind Zone (3, F6)
Grindwear, streetwear and footwear (big range of Soap shoes) for skaters and grinders. This bit of Granville Rd is a top strip for easy heads-or-tails fashion and coordinates.
✉ 32a Granville Rd, Tsim Sha Tsui ☎ 2545 7732 ⊕ Tsim Sha Tsui 🚌 5, 5c, 8, 8a ⊘ noon-10pm

Kent & Curwen
(4, G9) Distinguished suits, dress shirts, cufflinks and casual tops for the gentleman who'd rather look to the manor born than dotcom upstart.
✉ Shop 372, Pacific Place, 88 Queensway, Admiralty ☎ 2840 0023 ⊕ Admiralty ⊘ 10am-7.30pm

Nat's (4, E5)
Streety clompers and sneakers in a tucked-away blue lightbox of a shop. All prices are pretty reasonable but large sizes are sold even cheaper – might be just the ticket for your plate-sized western feet.
✉ Shop G2, Melbourne Plaza, 33 Queen's Rd Central, Central ☎ 2524 3980 ⊕ Central ⚓ Star Ferry ⊘ Mon-Sat 10am-7.30pm, Sun 10.30am-7pm

Pro Cam-Fis (3, J2)
Outdoor gear, both lightweight and cold weather, including kids' sizes. There's a good range of Eagle Creek travel products.
✉ Shop 148, Ocean Terminal, Harbour City, Canton Rd, Tsim Sha Tsui ☎ 2736 1382 ⊕ Tsim Sha Tsui ⚓ Star Ferry ⊘ 10am-7pm

Rag Brochure (2, B2)
One of a crush of fashion outlets selling new and

Emporio Armani suit you?

vintage gear for guys and gals. This is where the cool dudes shop for clothes, cheap jewellery, watches and action figures.
✉ Shop 4, Chow Tai Fook Centre/Trendy Zone, 580a Nathan Rd, Mong Kok ☎ 2391 4660 ⊕ Mong Kok/Yau Ma Tei ⊘ 2-10.30pm

ST Dupont (3, J5)
Everything for the wannabe French *gentilhomme*: suits, shirts, casual wear, belts, smoking accessories and briefcases.
✉ Shop BW7, The Peninsula, Salisbury Rd, Tsim Sha Tsui ☎ 2721 1998 ⊕ Tsim Sha Tsui ⚓ Star Ferry ⊘ Mon-Sat 10am-7pm

Fashionistas & Outlet Hounds

Hong Kong pretties up for Fashion Week in mid-July. The main parades and events are at the Convention & Exhibition Centre but look out for well-dressed shindigs in shopping centres around town.

If you are shopping at the other end of the scale, snap up *The Smart Shopper in Hong Kong* by Carolyn Radin to help you bargain hunt.

FOR CHILDREN

Goody Toys (4, D6)
Small but select range of high-quality playthings including plenty of educational toys and some that are a plain old lark.
✉ Shop 2033, IFC Mall, 1 Harbour View St, Central ☎ 2295 0552 ⊖ Central ⚓ Star Ferry 🚇 Hong Kong Station ⊘ 10am-8pm

Mothercare (4, E6)
Baby gear, supplies for mums and dads (prams, bouncers, bottles), plus toys for tots. Most of the stock is imported from Europe.
✉ Shop 338, Prince's Bldg, 10 Chater Rd, Central ☎ 2523 5704 ⊖ Central ⚓ Star Ferry ⊘ 10am-6pm

Stanley Market: tiny clothes at tiny prices (see p. 41)

Ocean Boutique (3, H6)
Kiddies gear made in China and Korea, much of it with funny English misspellings. The jumpsuits promise rumpus while the formal dresses are both tragic and gigglesome.
✉ 1 Minden Ave, Tsim

Children love the Toy Museum too.

Sha Tsui ☎ 2366 0889 ⊖ Tsim Sha Tsui 🚌 5, 5c, 8, 8a ⊘ Mon-Sat 10am-7pm

Toto cotton at Toto

Toto (4, E6)
Jumpsuits and other togs for under-2s; everything made by this Hong Kong brand is 100% cotton.
✉ Shop 212, Prince's Bldg, 10 Chater Rd, Central ☎ 2869 4668 ⊖ Central ⚓ Star Ferry ⊘ 10am-7pm

Toy Museum (4, E6)
Top-of-the-line teddy bears, action men, beanie babies and Pokemon paraphernalia. There's a great collection of old GI Joes for dads to amuse themselves with.
✉ Shop 320, Prince's Bldg, 10 Chater Rd, Central ☎ 2869 9138 ⊖ Central ⚓ Star

Ferry ⊘ Mon-Sat 10am-7pm, Sun noon-7pm

Wise Kids (4, G9)
Nothing to plug in, nothing with batteries: Wise Kids concentrates on kids generating energy with their necktop unit. As well as stuffed toys, card games and things to build, there are practical items for parents like toilet-lid locks and carry-alls.
✉ Shop 134, Pacific Place, 88 Queensway, Admiralty ☎ 2868 0133 ⊖ Admiralty ⊘ 10.30am-7.30pm

Hong Kong kids know how to frock up in style.

JEWELLERY & COSMETICS

Amours Antiques
(6, C2) Twentieth-century wearable antiques like rhinestone jewellery, frocks and a darling clutch of beaded and tapestry bags. Most wares date from 1910-40. A second branch holds forth in the Galleria (9 Queen's Rd Central).
✉ 45 Staunton St, Soho ☎ 2803 7877 ⊕ Central/Sheung Wan ✆ ⏰ Mon-Sat 2-8pm

Georg Jensen (3, J5)
Jensen's specialises in expertly crafted silver. The jewellery is exquisite, but it's in the liquid-looking ornaments and perfectly weighted cutlery that the Danish designer's imagination really seems to spark.
✉ Shop BL2, The Peninsula, Salisbury Rd, Tsim Sha Tsui ☎ 2724 1510 ⊕ Tsim Sha Tsui ⚓ Star Ferry ⏰ 10am-6.30pm (Sun from 11am)

J's (3, J2)
Affordable jewellery for those who like to gleam without being ostentatious. Most pieces are silver but some feature small diamonds; there's a groovy range of sunglasses. There are a dozen stores in town.
✉ Shop 231d, Ocean Terminal, Harbour City, Canton Rd, Tsim Sha Tsui ☎ 2803 8593 ⊕ Tsim Sha Tsui ⚓ Star Ferry ⏰ 10am-7pm

King Fook (4, D5)
The most fantastic-looking store in the reputable King Fook jewellery chain is worth visiting for its sheer garishness. There are branches in Admiralty (Shop 216, Pacific Place),

Causeway Bay (HK Mansion, 1 Yee Wo St) and Tsim Sha Tsui (Miramar Hotel, 118-130 Nathan Rd).
✉ 30-32 Des Voeux Rd, Central ☎ 2822 8573 ⊕ Central ⚓ Star Ferry ⎘ Hong Kong Station ⏰ 9.30am-7pm

Diamonds are a Hong Kong gal's best pal.

King Sing Jewellers
(3, J3) A long-standing jewellers with a wide selection of diamonds, pearls and gold items. The sales staff are pleasantly un-pushy.
✉ Shop 14, Star House, 3 Salisbury Rd, Tsim Sha Tsui ☎ 2735 7021 ⊕ Tsim Sha Tsui ⚓ Star Ferry ⏰ 10am-7.30pm

Premier Jewellery
(3, H5) Third-generation family firm directed by a qualified gemmologist. The selection isn't huge but if you're looking for something particular, give them a day's notice to have a selection ready for your arrival. Henry Cheng and team will also help you create your own designs.
✉ Shop G16, Holiday Inn Golden Mile, 50 Nathan Rd, Tsim Sha Tsui ☎ 2368 0003 ⊕ Tsim Sha Tsui ⚓ Star Ferry ⏰ Mon-Sat 10am-7.30pm, Sun 10.30am-4pm

Shu Uemura Beauty Boutique (4, G9)
The place to come for mauve eyelashes, spangly nail polish and rust lipstick as well as a deluxe range of make-up brushes, soothing bath tonics and skincare advice. There are branches in The Landmark and Times Square.
✉ Shop 129, Pacific Place, 88 Queensway, Admiralty ☎ 2918 1238 ⊕ Admiralty ⏰ 10.30am-8pm

Mauled by the Malls?
Hong Kong's most exciting fashion is hidden in unlikely looking commercial buildings. Catch a ride to the 4th floor, Rise Building (3, F6), 5-11 Granville Circuit, Tsim Sha Tsui, for tiny shops like **OI** (bright pinks and girly layers) and **Zimmone** (fun jewellery like jube earrings and spangly necklaces). The Beverley Commercial Centre (3, F7), 87-105 Chatham Rd, Tsim Sha Tsui, has a happy rash of fashion faves: **Pomp London** (11th floor) sells platform rave shoes. In Causeway Bay, Island Beverley (5, E3), 1 Great George St, is a good place to nose out young designer output. Early birds don't catch these worms: opening hours are around 3-10pm.

BOOKS

Angelo de Carpi

(6, C4) Nominally gay and lesbian bookshop but much more of a boyzone than a lady-lover lounge. Blokes should find this cellar-like space a comfortable hangout – as well as the books and vids, there are chatty little tables set against a fetching fake creeper wall.
✉ 18 Wo On Lane, Lan Kwai Fong, ☎ 2857 7148 ⊙ Central
⊙ Tues-Sun noon-9pm

Bookazine scene

Bookazine (4, E6)

Operates atmosphere-free chain stores dotted all around Hong Kong. Each shop stocks a dependable range of books, magazines and stationery.
✉ Shop 327-329, Prince's Bldg, 10 Chater Rd, Central ☎ 2522 1785 ⊙ Central
🚢 Star Ferry ⊙ Mon-Sat 9am-7pm, Sun 10am-6pm

Cosmos Books

(4, G11) Has a good selection of Chinese-related books in the basement. Upstairs there are English-language books (nonfiction is quite strong) plus one of the city's best stationery departments.
✉ 30 Johnston Rd, Wan Chai ☎ 2866

1677 ⊙ Wan Chai
🚊 🚌 37b, 75, 90
⊙ 10am-8pm

Dymocks (4, D6)

Australia's Dymocks chain offers a solid mainstream selection of page-turners, travel books and mags. There's a smaller branch in Central's Star Ferry concourse.
✉ Shop 2007-2011, IFC Mall, 1 Harbour View St, Central
☎ 2117 0360 ⊙ Central 🚢 Star Ferry
🚇 Hong Kong Station
⊙ Mon-Sat 9am-9pm, Sun 10am-8.30pm

Hong Kong Book Centre (4, D5)

This basement shop has a vast selection of books and magazines, including a mammoth number of business titles. There's another pleasantly cluttered branch in the basement of The Landmark.
✉ On Lok Yuen Bldg, 25 Des Voeux Rd Central, Central ☎ 2522 7064 ⊙ Central 🚢 Star Ferry 🚇 Hong Kong Station ⊙ Mon-Fri 9am-6.30pm, Sat 9am-5.30pm, Sun (summer only) 1-5pm

Joint Publishing Company (6, A5)

Joint Publishing (opposite the Central Market) is outstanding for books about China and books and tapes for studying Chinese languages. Most English titles, including the patchy but creditable literature section, are on the mezzanine.
✉ 9 Queen Victoria St, Central ☎ 2868 6844
⊙ Central 🚢 Star Ferry ⊙ Mon-Fri

10.30am-7.30pm, Sat 11am-9pm, Sun 1-6pm

Kelly & Walsh

(4, G9) A smart store with a good selection of art, design and culinary books. The children's books are shelved in a handy kids' reading lounge.
✉ Shop 304, Pacific Place, 88 Queensway, Admiralty ☎ 2522 5743 ⊙ Admiralty
⊙ Mon-Sat 9.30am-8pm, Sun 11am-8pm

Page One (3, J3)

A chain, yes, but one with attitude. Page One has Hong Kong's best selection of art and design magazines and books; it's also strong on photography, literature, film and children's books. There's another big branch in Festival Walk, Kowloon Tong (lower ground; cafe on site).
✉ Shop 3002, Harbour City, Canton Rd, Tsim Sha Tsui ☎ 2730 6080
⊙ Tsim Sha Tsui
🚢 Star Ferry ⊙ Sun-Thurs noon-10pm, Fri-Sat noon-10.30pm

Park Bookstore

(2, B2) Mostly Chinese gay literature, videos and VCDs, mainly for guys. Once you've found the narrow building entrance, walk all the way to the back and up the stairs.
✉ Rex House, 648 Nathan Rd, Mong Kok ☎ 2787 7988
⊙ Mong Kok 🚌 1, 1a, 6, 6a ⊙ 11.30am-9pm

Professional Bookshop (4, E6)

This shop carries an excellent selection of business,

Recommended Reading

One of the best history books is Jan Morris' *Hong Kong – Epilogue to an Empire*. *The Last Governor* is Jonathan Dimbleby's acclaimed account of Chris Patten's historic mission to Hong Kong. *Culture Shock! Hong Kong – A Guide to Customs and Etiquette* by Betty Wei and Elizabeth Li is an excellent introduction to Hong Kong culture. Edward Stokes' *Exploring Hong Kong's Countryside* is a good resource for hikers and nature-lovers. The most famous novel set in Hong Kong is *The World of Suzie Wong*, written in 1957 by Richard Mason and set in seedy Wan Chai. *Planet Hong Kong: Popular Cinema and the Art of Entertainment* is David Bordwell's somewhat academic investigation of the art and culture of Hong Kong movies.

legal and professional titles. It's a good place to get grounded in business-speak, Hong Kong style.

⊠ **Shop 104a, Alexandra House, 16-20 Chater Rd, Central** ☎ **2526 5387** Ⓒ **Central** ⚓ **Star Ferry** ◷ **Mon-Fri 9am-6.30pm, Sat 9am-5.30pm**

Swindon Books

(3, H4) Swindon, behind the Hyatt Regency, is one of Hong Kong's larger booksellers. There are branches in Harbour City (Deck 2, Ocean Terminal, and Shops 310 & 328, Ocean Centre), and another at the Star Ferry Terminal in Tsim Sha Tsui.

⊠ **13-15 Lock Rd, Tsim Sha Tsui** ☎ **2366 8001** Ⓒ **Tsim Sha Tsui** ◷ **Mon-Thurs 9am-6.30pm, Fri-Sat 9am-7.30pm, Sun 12.30-6.30pm**

Tai Yip Art Book Centre **(6, C4)**

A terrific selection of books about anything Chinese and arty: calligraphy, jade, bronze, costumes, architecture – it's all here in force. This is a good place to look a little deeper if you're planning on buying art in Hong Kong; it's also a good place for picking up beautiful gift cards. There's a branch in the Museum of Art, cnr Nathan & Salisbury Rds, Tsim Sha Tsui.

⊠ **72 Wellington St, Lan Kwai Fong** ☎ **2524 5963** Ⓒ **Central** ◷ **Mon-Fri 10am-7pm, Sat-Sun 10am-6.30pm**

MUSIC

CD Exchange of Hong Kong **(2, B2)**

Elevator-sized store crammed in a muggy basement full of CD outlets. While most dispense Cantopop, CD Exchange stocks alternative pop and – radically – sells secondhand as well as new discs. **Mini Shop** nearby sells poppy dance and soundtracks (Shop B1).

⊠ **Shop B8, Sino Centre, 582-592 Nathan Rd, Mong Kok** ☎ **2782 1692** Ⓒ **Mong Kok/Yau Ma Tei** ▤ **1, 1a, 2, 6, 6a** ◷ **1-9pm**

HMV **(4, E5)**

If you're not after anything too obscure, HMV will probably satisfy with its good range of CDs, DVDs and magazines. There are branches in Causeway Bay (Windsor House, 311 Gloucester Rd) and Tsim Sha Tsui (Sands Bldg, 12 Peking Rd).

⊠ **Central Bldg, 1-3 Pedder St, Central** ☎ **2739 0268** Ⓒ **Central** ⚓ **Star Ferry** ◷ **9am-10pm**

Hong Kong Records **(4, G9)** Local outfit with a good selection of Cantonese and international sounds including Chinese traditional music, jazz, classical and composer music. There's also a good range of VCDs, both Chinese and western movies (with Chinese subtitles).

⊠ **Shop 252, Pacific Place, 88 Queensway, Admiralty** ☎ **2845 7088** Ⓒ **Admiralty** ◷ **10am-8pm (Thurs-Sat till 9pm)**

Plug **(6, D5)**

Hong Kong's only dedicated independent music store is a modest enthusiast-run operation which specialises in indie and imported sounds you wouldn't even bother asking for anywhere else.

⊠ **58 D'Aguilar St, Lan Kwai Fong** ☎ **2809 4603** Ⓒ **Central** ◷ **Mon-Fri 10am-6pm, Sat noon-4pm**

FOOD & TOBACCO

Aji Ichiban (4, D6)
One of a chain of shops selling exotic dried fruit (sour plum, 10-scent olive) and the freaky dried seafood you see at the markets, but here with English labels (shredded squid, eel slices) and nibble-sized tasting portions.
✉ Shop 2001, IFC Mall, 1 Harbour View St, Central ☎ 2868 9916 Ⓜ Central 🚢 Star Ferry 🚉 Hong Kong Station ⏱ 10am-7pm

CitySuper (5, G2)
Gourmet supermarket with ready-to-eats like sushi and salads and lots of fresh produce flown in at exorbitant prices. Even if you're not shopping, you can browse and be glad you're not paying $60 for a bunch of leeks back home. Also Level 3, Harbour City, Tsim Sha Tsui.
✉ Times Square, 1 Matheson St, Causeway Bay ☎ 2506 2888 Ⓜ Causeway Bay ⏱ 10.30am-10pm (Fri-Sat till 11pm)

Fook Ming Tong Tea Shop (4, E5)
Carefully chosen teas and tea-making accoutrements. There's tea of various ages and propensities, even a 'solitary tea' which tastes appropriately bitter. There are other stores, including one in the Sogo department store, Causeway Bay, and another in Ocean Terminal, Harbour City (Shop 124).
✉ Shop G3-4, The Landmark, 1 Pedder St, Central ☎ 2521 0337 Ⓜ Central 🚢 Star Ferry ⏱ Mon-Sat 10am-7.30pm, Sun 11am-6pm

Lock Cha Tea Shop (4, D2) Our favourite shop (enter from Ladder St) for Chinese teas, tea sets, wooden tea boxes and well-presented gift packs of various cuppas. You can try before you buy.
✉ 290a Queen's Rd Central, Sheung Wan ☎ 2805 1360 Ⓜ Sheung Wan 🚌 26 ⏱ 11am-7pm

Lock Cha Tea to a T

Minamoto Kitchoan (6, C4) These folk go to unbelievable bother to make sweets so intricate that eating them seems crude. Do it anyway and try the *tousenka* (a big peach whose stone is replaced by a baby green peach).
✉ Shop B, Winway Bldg, 50 Wellington St,

Central ☎ 2577 5702 Ⓜ Central ⏱ Mon-Sat 10am-9pm, Sun 10am-8pm

Oliver's (4, E6)
The wood-panelled floors set the tone: this ain't no ordinary supermarket. Matzos or Mexican hot sauce? Got it. There's also a great range of international beers and the imported fruit and vegies obviously come first class.
✉ Shop 233-237, Prince's Bldg, 10 Chater Rd, Central ☎ 2869 5119 Ⓜ Central 🚢 Star Ferry 🚉 Hong Kong Station ⏱ 9am-8pm

Tabaqueria Filipina (4, E6) Sometimes you do need a fat cigar to feel like you're making it in the big city. This boxy store comes to the rescue with Cuban, Dominican and other fine chompers. There are other branches at 30 Wyndham St, Central and Convention Plaza, Wan Chai.
✉ Shop 105, Alexandra Bldg, 6 Ice House St, Central ☎ 2877 1541 Ⓜ Central 🚢 Star Ferry ⏱ Mon-Fri 10am-7.30pm, Sat 10am-6.30pm

Dried fish: guaranteed to stink up your luggage

COMPUTERS & ELECTRONICS

Chung Yuen Electrical Co (4, E6)
Fair-minded, fixed-price electronics store with a good selection of DVD players, sound systems, monitors and organisers. The shop is small but the gear is good.
✉ **Shop 227, Prince's Bldg, 10 Chater Rd, Central** ☎ **2524 8066** ⓖ **Central** ⛴ **Star Ferry** ⏰ **10am-7pm**

Houston Crest (3, J3) Slick collection of desktops, laptops and PDAs, but for many travellers it will be the accessories which prove handy. Modem protectors, various adaptors and cables could

An apple a day...
Hong Kong Tourist Association

be what you need to get roadworthy. There are outlets in Harbour City and Causeway Bay (Windsor House, 311 Gloucester Rd).
✉ **Shop D1, Star House, 3 Salisbury Rd, Tsim Sha Tsui** ☎ **2730 4382** ⓖ **Tsim Sha Tsui** ⛴ **Star Ferry** ⏰ **10am-6pm**

IT Pulse Point (3, G6)
One of the shops in the sparkling CyberCity computer arcade, IT Pulse Point has a reasonable selection of desktops, motherboards, monitors and PDAs. There are another dozen or so stores to browse here.
✉ **Shop 14, Railway Plaza, 29 Chatham Rd South, Tsim Sha Tsui** ☎ **2724 8678** ⓖ **Tsim Sha Tsui** 🚌 **5, 5c, 8, 8a** ⏰ **10am-7pm**

Winframe System (2, B2) This is just one of your options in the Mong Kok Computer Centre – three floors packed with

Circuitry Circus
The **Golden Building Shopping Centre**, 146-152 Fuk Wah St, Sham Shui Po (2, A2; take exit D from the MTR and it's right across the street), is the place for cheap software of somewhat dubious origin, games and accessories like mice, keyboards, printer cartridges and disks. Most shops open daily 10am-9pm but some don't open till noon. It's packed on weekends.

shops selling software and hardware: modems, processors, digital cameras, disk drives, laptops, computer manuals.
✉ **Shop 106, Mong Kok Computer Centre, 8 Nelson St, Mong Kok** ☎ **2300 1238** ⓖ **Mong Kok** ⏰ **1-10pm**

PHOTOGRAPHIC EQUIPMENT

Color Six (6, C5)
Reliable photo processing (slides take just three hours) and professional film for sale. Prices aren't the lowest in town but the service is top quality.
✉ **Shell Bldg, 18a**

Lights, cameras, action!
John Hay

Stanley St, Lan Kwai Fong ☎ **2542 2677** ⓖ **Central** ⏰ **Mon-Fri 8am-7pm, Sat 8am-5pm**

Hing Lee Camera Company (6, B3)
Hing Lee is a reputable photographic supply outlet. Come here for new and second-hand 35mm camera bodies and lenses and mid-range compact cameras.
✉ **25 Lyndhurst Tce, Lan Kwai Fong** ☎ **2544 7593** ⓖ **Central** ↘ ⏰ **Mon-Sat 9.30am-7pm**

Photo Scientific (6, C5) This is the favourite of Hong Kong's resident professional photographers. You might find some equipment elsewhere for less, but Photo Scientific has a rock-solid reputation, with labelled prices, no bargaining, no arguing and no cheating.
✉ **Eurasia Bldg, 6 Stanley St, Lan Kwai Fong** ☎ **2522 1903** ⓖ **Central** ⏰ **Mon-Sat 10am-7pm**

SPORTING EQUIPMENT

Ahluwalia & Sons
(3, H4) Shabby but long-established and well-stocked store flogging golf gear, tennis racquets, cricket bats, shirts and balls. It's cash only and no prices are marked – what further incitement to haggle do you need?
✉ 8c Hankow Rd, Tsim Sha Tsui ☎ 2368 8334
🚇 Tsim Sha Tsui
⛴ Star Ferry
⏰ 10am-7.30pm

Wise Mount Sports Co (2, B2)
Wise Mount Sport is a long-standing family-run store with camping gear, swimming goggles, pocketknives, compasses, hard-wearing bags and even sports trophies.
✉ 75 Sai Yee St, Mong Kok ☎ 2787 3011
🚇 Mong Kok
⏰ noon-10pm

World Top (4, F6)
This smallish shop is crammed with 18 holes worth of golf gear plus a bonus round of tennis racquets.
✉ Shop 212, The Galleria, 9 Queen's Rd Central, Central
☎ 2521 3703
🚇 Central ⛴ Star Ferry
⏰ Mon-Sat 9.30am-6.45pm, Sun 10am-6pm

Zoom (2, B2)
Superfly treads rule in this teasing strip of sports-shoe shops. All brands and breeds of sneakers get air, get swoosh and get going along here. It's packed on weekends.
✉ 65 Fa Yuen St, Mong Kok ☎ 2781 0920 🚇 Mong Kok
⏰ 11.30am-11pm

ANTIQUES & FURNISHINGS

Heavenly antiques

Arch Angel Antiques
(6, B2) Though the specialities are antique and reproduction porcelain and tombware, Arch Angel packs a lot more into its three floors: there's everything from mahjong sets to terracotta horses to palatial furniture. You'll feel as comfortable here buying a small gift as a feature ornament for the salon.
✉ 53-55 Hollywood Rd, Central
☎ 2851 6828
🚇 Central/Sheung Wan
🚌 26 ⏰ 9.30am-6.30pm

Caravan (6, B2)
Trustworthy rug-sellers travel all over Asia to stock this nicely cluttered shop. The range of Afghan and Tibetan carpets is especially notable. among a varied rug range.
✉ 65 Hollywood Rd, Central ☎ 2547 3821
🚇 Central/Sheung Wan
🚌 26 ⏰ 10am-7pm

Chine Gallery (6, C3)
Carefully restored furniture (we love the lacquered cabinets) from all over China and hand-knotted rugs from remote regions like Xinjiang, Ningxia, Gansu and Inner Mongolia. All items are sourced by two brothers, Zafar and Anwer Islam, who own the shop and oversee the

Carpet flies out the door at caravan.

Chine Gallery

restoration.
✉ 42a Hollywood Rd,
Central ☎ 2543 0023
Ⓜ Central/Sheung Wan
🚌 26 ⏰ Mon-Sat
10am-7pm, Sun 1-6pm

Chinese Carpet Centre Ltd (3, J3)

You'll be floored by the huge selection of new carpets and rugs, most of them made in China but some from as far away as France.
✉ Shop 178, Ocean Terminal, Harbour City, Canton Rd, Tsim Sha Tsui ☎ 2735 1030
Ⓜ Tsim Sha Tsui
⛴ Star Ferry
⏰ 10am-7pm

Hobbs & Bishops Fine Art (6, C3)

Waxy-smelling shop specialising in lacquered wooden furniture from 19th-century northern China. Their eye tends more to sleekly handsome than ostentatious pieces.
✉ 28 Hollywood Rd,
Central ☎ 2537 9838
Ⓜ Central 🚌 26
⏰ Mon-Sat 10am-6pm

Karin Weber Antiques (6, C2)

An enjoyable mix of Chinese country antiques and contemporary Asian artworks. The folk here give short lectures on antiques and the scene in Hong Kong and provide shopping services for serious, focused buyers.
✉ 32a Staunton St,
Soho ☎ 2544 5004
Ⓜ Central/Sheung Wan
🔧 ⏰ Mon-Sat 11am-7pm

Mir Oriental Carpets (6, D4)

Wall-to-wall-to-ceiling carpets mostly from Iran. The antique carpets are exquisite and expensive; the new carpets warp and weft from repro to hip.
✉ New India House,
52 Wyndham St,
Central ☎ 2521 5641
Ⓜ Central 🚌 26
⏰ Mon-Sat 10am-7pm,
Sun 11am-5pm

Schoeni Fine Oriental Art (6, C3)

This Swiss company has been in Hong Kong for over 20 years. It specialises in 17th- to 19th-century Chinese antique furniture and South-East Asian ceramics.
✉ Hollywood House,
27 Hollywood Rd,
Central ☎ 2542 3143
Ⓜ Central ⏰ Mon-Sat
10am-6pm

Tai Sing Company (4, E5)

Tai Sing has been selling quality Chinese antiques for 50 years with a special focus on porcelain. Two of the shop's six floors are now devoted to European furniture including a dandy assembly of Art Deco pieces.
✉ 12 Wyndham St,
Central ☎ 2525 9365
Ⓜ Central
⏰ Mon-Sat 10am-6pm

Tibetan Gallery (6, D4)

This small showroom heads a string of antique and reproduction stores in the Yu Yuet Lai Bldg. In this one you'll find authentic Tibetan artefacts from rugs to mini-altars.
✉ Yu Yuet Lai Bldg,
55 Wyndham St,
Central ☎ 2530 4863
Ⓜ Central 🚌 26
⏰ Mon-Sat 10.30am-7.30pm, Sun noon-6pm

Many a beautiful thing

Go and Get It...

Karin Weber (see above) leads two-day trips to her company's warehouse in northwest Guangdong. Not only do you get to trawl through the massive selection of original and restored antiques, available at a smidgen over the wholesale price, you get a taste of a little-touristed part of China. The charge of $2100/person means there's no obligation to buy.

SOUVENIRS & GIFTS

Design Gallery
(4, D12) Supported by the Hong Kong Trade Development Council, this shop showcases local design in the form of jewellery, toys, ornaments and gadgets. This rationale for a shop results in a somewhat chaotic – but often rewarding – gaggle of goodies.
✉ **Hong Kong Convention & Exhibition Centre, 1 Harbour Rd, Wan Chai** ☎ **2584 4146** Ⓜ **Wan Chai** ⚓ **Star Ferry** ⏰ **10am-7pm**

King & Country
(4, G9) Models and miniatures, mostly of a military bent (the American War of Independence, and so forth). There are also street models of old Hong Kong: building frontages, a Chinese wedding procession, even an 'amah (maid) with baby and chicken'.
✉ **Shop 362, Pacific Place, 88 Queensway, Admiralty** ☎ **2525 8603** Ⓜ **Admiralty** ⏰ **Mon-Sat 10.30am-8pm, Sun noon-6pm**

Liuligongfang
(4, E5) Exquisite coloured objects, both practical (glasses, bowls, vases and candle holders) and ornamental (figurines, crystal Buddhas, breathtaking sculptures) can be found in abundance here. Everything comes from the one design studio and workshop in China.
✉ **Shop 20-22, Central Bldg, 1-3 Pedder St, Central** ☎ **2973 0820** Ⓜ **Central** ⚓ **Star Ferry** ⏰ **10am-7.30pm**

Mandarin Oriental Flower & Gift Shop
(4, E6) Crockery, cushion covers, chopsticks, tasteful souvenirs and a small selection of jewellery will appeal whether you're looking for gifts or treats for yourself.
✉ **Shop 13-14, Mandarin Oriental Hotel, 5 Connaught Rd, Central** ☎ **2840 1974** Ⓜ **Central** ⚓ **Star Ferry** ⏰ **Mon-Fri 9am-7pm, Sat 9am-6pm, Sun 10am-5pm**

Geniune articles at Fai Kee, Sheung Wan

Mountain Folkcraft
(6, C5) One of the nicest stores in town for folk crafts. This place has batiks, clothing, woodcarvings and lacquerware made by ethnic minorities in China and other Asian countries. The shop attendants are friendly, and prices, while not cheap, are not outrageous either.
✉ **15 Wo On Lane, Lan Kwai Fong** ☎ **2525 3199** Ⓜ **Central** 🚌 **13, 26, 43** ⏰ **Mon-Sat 9.30am-6.30pm**

Stone Village (2, B2)
Creative plant pots, pottery figurines and tea sets plus a lot of beautiful bonsai that you're unfortunately unlikely to be able to take home.
✉ **44 Flower Market Rd, Mong Kok** ☎ **2787 0218** Ⓜ **Prince Edward** 🚌 **1, 1a, 2c, 12a** ⏰ **9.30am-7.30pm**

Yue Hwa (3, F5)
There are five Yue Hwa stores in Hong Kong, but this is the brightest and biggest. It's one-stop shopping Chinese style: bolts of silk, herbs, clothes, porcelain, luggage, umbrellas, kitchenware – it's all here.
✉ **Park Lane, 143-161 Nathan Rd, Tsim Sha Tsui** ☎ **2739 3888** Ⓜ **Jordan** ⚓ **Star Ferry** ⏰ **10am-10pm**

It's easy to get shirty in Hong Kong.

places to eat

There's a saying that the only four-legged thing a Cantonese person won't eat is a table. Observation suggests that the only flying object deemed inedible is an aeroplane and anything underwater is fair game unless it's wearing a swimsuit. This collective passion for eating makes Hong Kong one of the world's great foodie cities – grab your chopsticks and tuck in.

Price Ranges

It's possible to eat very cheaply in Hong Kong by following the locals into soup and noodle restaurants. More sophisticated Chinese, other Asian and Western-food restaurants are usually quite expensive. Keep in mind that lots of restaurants have value-priced set lunches.

The price scale below represents the cost of an average dinner with a glass of wine.

$	under $50
$$	$51-149
$$$	$150-350
$$$$	over $350

Simon Rowe

Cuisines

Most of Hong Kong's 10,000 restaurants are Chinese. Cantonese is the home-town cuisine but Chiu Chow and Shanghainese food is also easy to find. Cantonese cuisine is famously fresh: there's an emphasis on fresh-killed meat, mostly pork and seafood. Simple techniques like steaming and stir-frying allow the ingredients to shine. Chiu Chow food makes liberal use of garlic, vinegar and sauces; it's famous for cold goose, crab and delicacies like shark's fin soup. Shanghainese cooking uses a lot more salted and preserved foods and depends on stewing, braising and frying. Dumplings and noodles are often eaten instead of rice.

Don't worry if you're having a bad noodle day. Hong Kong is an international city and you're liable to see bangers 'n mash, lasagne and croque-monsieur before there's time to say 'beef tendon congee'. The highest concentration of Western restaurants is in Soho and Lan Kwai Fong. Every neighbourhood is studded with cheap and mid-range Chinese restaurants – take a turn off the main streets to find plenty of bustling noodle bars. The top Chinese restaurants are in hotels – there's no shame in heading to a hotel restaurant for a special meal.

Hong Kong Tourist Association

Food so fresh it crawls on to your plate.

Etiquette

Eating out is usually a casual affair but there are a few points of etiquette it doesn't hurt to keep in mind. Top-end restaurants require smart casual dress: sports shoes and shorts may not be acceptable. Men can forego a tie – a collared shirt will suffice. If eating in a group, wait for some signal from your host before digging in. When eating rice, hold the bowl near your lips and shovel the contents into your mouth with chopsticks. Don't stick your chopsticks upright into your rice – this is how rice is offered to the dead, and the connotations at meal time are not pleasant for Chinese people. And don't worry if you spill food on the tablecloth – eating in groups, especially dim sum, is a joyfully messy affair.

> ## Tea Top-Up
> When you need a tea refill in a Chinese restaurant, you signal the waiter by taking the lid slightly off the teapot. When tea is served you can thank the waiter by tapping your middle finger lightly on the table.

Hong Kong Tourist Association

Tea for two, or three

Drinks

The typical liquid accompaniment to Chinese food is tea – it's drunk from the meal's beginning to end from a periodically refilled pot. Beer is available almost everywhere but wine doesn't start to feature until you're in mid- to upper-range places. Top Chinese restaurants pay great attention to their wine lists but the mark-ups are savage. Western restaurants tend to have small, unexciting lists with a couple of reasonable tipples available by the glass.

Booking & Tipping

In all but the cheapies, it's advisable to book ahead, especially on Friday and Saturday nights. Most restaurants add a 10% service charge. In cheap to mid-price restaurants, you can consider this a tip. In expensive restaurants, it's assumed you'll tip up to 10% on top of the service charge.

> ## Tasty Views
> If you're a sucker for a view, you're going to love Hong Kong. The best ground-level views are looking back across the harbour from Tsim Sha Tsui, most notably from **Yu** (3, K5; ☎ 2721 1211; $$$$), the topnotch seafood restaurant in the waterfront Regent Hotel.
>
> On the island side, the best views are from on high. **R66** (4, H12; ☎ 2862 6166; $$$), 62nd fl, Hopewell Centre, 183 Queen's Rd East, Wan Chai, obeys the unwritten code of revolving restaurants by playing cheesy music, serving average buffets and meals with a surf 'n' turf angle. It's best to roll up for an afternoon coffee or a fruity cocktail and go for a spin. To go up in the outfacing bubble lifts change at the 17th floor (lifts 27 and 28 in the alcove opposite lift 6).
>
> If you want a bit more class, try **Scenario** (4, D4; ☎ 2186 6868; $$$), 42nd fl, The Center, 99 Queen's Rd Central, Central. The food is classic Italian but you can sit in the lounge for a drink and a snack.
>
> Other good-for-gawping restaurants are those at the Peak (p. 81), **Spring Moon** (p. 80), **Felix** (p. 78) and **Port Cafe** (p. 83).

ADMIRALTY & CENTRAL

City Hall Chinese Restaurant
(4, E7) **$$**
Chinese, Cantonese
This crazily busy dim sum restaurant has great harbour views but everyone's too busy eating to gaze outside. The dim sum comes by on wheelie carts and the morsels are adequately explained by the servers. Arrive before noon if you want to avoid queuing with office groups and wedding parties.
✉ **Low Block, City Hall, 7 Edinburgh Pl** ☎ **2521 1303** ⊕ **Central**
🚢 **Star Ferry** ⊙ **10am-3pm, 5.30-11pm** ♿ **yes**

You can't beat City Hall.

John Hay

Dai Pai Dong
(6, A3) **$**
Chinese, Hong Kong snacks
This modern version of the outdoor snack stand serves breakfast (bacon and eggs, porridge, instant noodles), lunch and dinner (noodles) but it's best to come at afternoon tea for *yuan yang* (half tea, half coffee), boiled cola with lemon and ginger and toast smeared with condensed milk.
✉ **128 Queen's Rd Central (also 70 Canton**

Rd, Tsim Sha Tsui; 20 Russell St, Causeway Bay) ☎ **2851 6389**
⊕ **Central** ⊙ **Mon-Sat 8am-10pm, Sun 9.30am-7pm (afternoon tea: 2.30-5.30pm)** ♿ **yes** **V**

Eating Plus
(4, D6) **$$**
International
Style comes cheap at this very vogue eatery and bar. Breakfasts are a snip (around $25) – omelettes are fluffy, juices are freshly squeezed. Lunch and dinner extend to soups, noodles (east and west) and risotto; reasonable set meals are available. Great health juices too.
✉ **Shop 1009, IFC Mall, 1 Harbour View St** ☎ **2868 0599**
⊕ **Central** 🚢 **Star Ferry** 🚆 **Airport Express** ⊙ **7.30am-10pm (till 8pm Sun)** ♿ **yes** **V**

Fat Heung Lam Vegetarian
(6, B4) **$**
Chinese, vegetarian
A small, friendly restaurant with a bilingual menu offering soups, tofu and noodles done about 100 different ways. If you're on the run, there's a window at the front where you can grab a snack.
✉ **94 Wellington St** ☎ **2543 0404**
⊕ **Central** ⊙ **11am-11pm** ♿ **yes** **V**

Fountainside
(4, E5) **$$$**
International
Freshly squeezed juices, good coffee and well-presented American breakfasts give way to grills and multi-culti you-say-noodle,

i-say-penne mains. The setting is the classy Landmark shopping centre with haute couture views – both walking and windowed.
✉ **Shop G6-7, The Landmark, 1 Pedder St** ☎ **2526 4018**
⊕ **Central** ⊙ **Mon-Fri 8am-9.30pm, Sat 8am-8pm, Sun 11am-7pm** **V**

Hunan Garden
(4, D5) **$$$**
Chinese, Hunanese
This elegant place in the Forum Mall specialises in spicy Hunanese cuisine. The fried chicken with chilli is excellent, as are the seafood dishes. The water-chestnut dumpling is a great sticky dessert. The views, overlooking the harbour or the heart of Central, are a bonus.
✉ **Forum Mall, Exchange Sq, 8 Connaught Pl** ☎ **2868 2880** ⊕ **Central** 🚢 **Star Ferry** 🚆 **Airport Express** ⊙ **11.30am-3pm, 5.30-11.30pm** **V**

Jimmy's Kitchen
(4, E5) **$$**
British, international
Jimmy's is big on nostalgia and, at 60 years of age, is one of the oldest restaurants in town. Although the emphasis is on British food, even the fussiest diner will appreciate the well-travelled menu. Specialities include char-grilled king prawns, baked onion soup and black pepper steak.
✉ **South China Bldg, 1-3 Wyndham St (also Kowloon Centre, 29 Ashley Rd, Tsim Sha Tsui)** ☎ **2526 5293**
⊕ **Central** ⊙ **noon-midnight**

Le Bistrot de Paris
(4, E5) $$$
French
This unpretentious French eatery richly deserves its popularity. Set dinners are available (from $250) if you'd prefer to get cosy in a booth than spend time hovering over the menu.
✉ 4-6 On Lan St (near Wyndham St) ☎ 2869 1132 Ⓜ Central ◷ 12.30-2.30pm, 6-11.30pm

Luk Yu Tea House
(6, C5) $$$
Chinese
Long-standing Luk Yu is a popular dim sum venue. This classy establishment with uncomfortable booths and grouchy elderly waiters is not the cheapest place (and the prices aren't marked), but the food is delicate and fresh.
✉ 24-26 Stanley St ☎ 2523 5464 Ⓜ Central ◷ 7am-10pm (dim sum until 5pm) ⅋ yes

Mughal Room
(6, D4) $$
Indian
Recommended Mughal Room dishes include the superb samosas, the *dahi papri* (lentil crisps covered with tamarind yoghurt sauce) and the *paneer dilbahar* (cream cheese and potato balls stuffed with dried fruit). The lunch buffet is excellent value.
✉ Carfield Commercial Bldg, 75-77 Wyndham St ☎ 2524 0107 Ⓜ Central ◷ noon-3pm, 6-11pm Ⓥ

The Square
(4, D6) $$$
Cantonese
This slick newcomer made a splash with stylish reworkings of Cantonese favourites. This is a good place to lash out on shark's fin soup. The hushed atmosphere and dedicated service make it a good choice for business or romance.
✉ Exchange Sq 2, 8 Connaught Pl ☎ 2525 1163 Ⓜ Central ◷ 11am-3pm, 6-11pm

Vong
(4, E6) $$$$
French, South-East Asian
Inside the Mandarin Oriental Hotel, dramatic Vong features a creative mix of Vietnamese, French and Thai food. Consider the tasting menu ($500) to get a full appreciation of the combination of French techniques with Asian flavours. Herbivores will appreciate the extensive vegetarian menu.
✉ Mandarin Oriental Hotel, 5 Connaught Rd ☎ 2825 4028 Ⓜ Central ◷ noon-3pm, 6pm-midnight (bar until 2am) Ⓥ

Business with a Bite
A lot of expense-account wining and dining occurs at hotel restaurants: in Tsim Sha Tsui consider the Hyatt's **Chinese Restaurant** (p. 78), and **Avenue** (3, H5; ☎ 2315 1118; $$$$) in the Holiday Inn Golden Mile, 50 Nathan Rd. On Hong Kong Island, the Renaissance Harbour View's **Dynasty** (p. 82) is right by the convention centre while **Vong** (below) in the Mandarin Oriental is as central as it gets.

Good lunch spots where you can talk without shouting include **Fountainside** (p. 70), **The Square** (below) and **Port Cafe** (p. 83). **Tables 88** (p. 77) and **Va Bene** (p. 72) are great places to take the team when you've sealed the deal.

Yè Shanghai
(4, G9) $$$
Chinese, Shanghainese
A newish player that takes street-level Shanghai cuisine and gives it a tweak here and there. The drunken pigeon is a wine-soaked winner and the steamed dumplings are perfectly plump, but sometimes this restaurant goes for clattery style over substance.
✉ Shop 332, Pacific Place, 88 Queensway ☎ 2918 9833 Ⓜ Admiralty ◷ 11.30am-3pm, 6-11.30pm Ⓥ

Yung Kee
(6, C5) $$$
Chinese
Hong Kong's reigning patriarch of Cantonese restaurants. The roast goose here has been the talk of the town since 1942, and its dim sum is also excellent. Though some say Yung Kee is resting on its laurels, there's plenty of return custom that deems otherwise.
✉ 32-40 Wellington St ☎ 2522 1624 Ⓜ Central ◷ 11am-11.30pm

LAN KWAI FONG

Beirut
(6, D5) $$$
Lebanese
A faux tavern where you can snack on hummus and bread washed down with beer or settle in with the gang for a whole sheep. The mixed grills are smoky and juicy and the service is pretty handy for such a bustling place.
✉ **Winner Bldg, 27-39 D'Aguilar St** ☎ **2804 6611** Ⓖ **Central** ⊘ **noon-12.30am** **V**

Chop Chop Café
(6, D5) $
American, international
The Chop Chop is a small, cheap eatery where you can fill up on baked potatoes, casseroles and other speedy cuisine. There are three good reasons to come here: you need beer soaker, you need it now and you need it cheap.
✉ **17 Wing Wah Lane** ☎ **2526 1122**

Ⓖ **Central** ⊘ **11.30am-11pm** ⚥ **yes** **V**

M at the Fringe
(6, E5) $$$$
International
No-one seems to have a bad thing to say about Michelle's, at the Fringe Club. The menus constantly change, but everything is excellent, whether it's ratatouille, couscous or kohlrabi. It's worth saving room for dessert, if you have that kind of self-restraint. Set lunches are available for $150. Reservations are a must.
✉ **South Block, 2 Lwr Albert Rd** ☎ **2877 4000** Ⓖ **Central** ⊘ **Mon-Fri noon-2.30pm, 7-10.30pm** **V**

Taste Good
(6, D5) $$
Thai, Cantonese
Upbeat cafe at the slops end of Lan Kwai Fong's charmingly nicknamed Rat

Alley. Simple, filling meat and vegetable curries come hot enough to raise a sweat; there are soups, noodles and more elaborate barbecued dishes too.
✉ **16 Wing Wah Lane** ☎ **2523 9543; 2522 4546** Ⓖ **Central** ⊘ **11am-1am** **V**

Va Bene
(6, D5) $$$
Italian
This smart restaurant bears a striking resemblance to a neighbourhood trattoria. Unusually for Hong Kong the house bread is excellent, but don't fill up before you get to the spaghetti or the lamb's shanks. It's a good choice for a special date or an extravagant celebration. Book ahead; dress smart.
✉ **58-62 D'Aguilar St** ☎ **2845 5577** Ⓖ **Central** ⊘ **noon-3pm, 7pm-midnight**

SOHO

Bayou
(6, C2) $$
American, Cajun
This Cajun joint has gone

down well with expats, who sit and get greasy on barbecue ribs while checking out who's who on the

escalator. It's a bit gimmicky (voodoo pasta) but this far from New Orleans y'all can't be too picky.
✉ **9-13 Shelley St** ☎ **2526 2118** Ⓖ **Central** ↘ ⊘ **8am-3pm, 6-11pm** **V**

Bistro Manchu
(6, C2) $$
Manchurian
Cosy and easy-going place specialising in myriad dumplings with dipping sauce (the cucumber and tofu combo is a vegetarian winner), plus soups and other three-bite snacks such as fried eggplant

Chasin' down that hoodoo meal at Bayou.

John Hay

Dai Pai Dong Gets the Gong

Hong Kong authorities are on a long campaign to clear the streets of dai pai dongs, the open-air street stalls selling noodles and snacks. New licences are not issued and there are restrictions about passing on current licences. This makes the noodle stands in Soho an endangered species – sit and slurp while you can.

stuffed with shredded pork. The pleasant dining room is red-themed with original (but not Manchurian) art.
⊠ **33 Elgin St** ☎ **2536 9218** Central ↖
⊘ noon-2pm, 6-10pm
V

Cubana
(6, D2) **$$$**
Cuban
Two-storey Cuban place with a good selection of tapas and serious cocktail pitchers. There's a barnyard of main dishes (pork, chicken, beef) plus a fish dish. The food is good, though a bit heavy for Hong Kong's humid summers, and the service can be tentative. There's live Cuban music and salsa dancing Thursday and Sunday.
⊠ **47b Elgin St**
☎ **2869 1218**
e hot4food@hkstar
.com Central ↖
⊘ noon-2am (lunch:

noon-2pm, dinner: 6pm-midnight)

Le Rendez-vous
(6, C3) **$**
French
Tiny nautically themed crepe house which also does baguettes and salads. The crepes come filled with classic combos like mushroom and cheese along with more adventurous spicy inventions. There's a full bar too with happy hour 6-8pm.
⊠ **5 Staunton St**
☎ **2905 1808**
Central ↖ ⊘ 10am-11.30pm ♿ yes **V**

Lin Heung Tea House
(4, D3) **$**
Chinese, Cantonese
Older-style Cantonese restaurant packed with old men reading the newspaper, families and office groups. There's OK dim sum (the food comes around on a trolley) but it's also recommended for a bite late at night. It's a very local place, but there is an English menu. Book ahead.
⊠ **160-164 Wellington St (cnr Aberdeen St)**
☎ **2544 4556**
Central ↖
⊘ 6am-11pm ♿ good

India Today
(6, C2) **$$**
Indian
India Today is a worthy player in the 'How many restaurants can you get on one block?' competition which has Elgin St in a frenzy. The curries are reasonably priced, the beer is icy and the atmosphere is pleasant.
⊠ **26-30 Elgin St**
☎ **2801 5959**
Central ↖
⊘ 11am-11pm **V**

Orange Tree
(6, D2) **$$$**
Dutch
Modern Dutch food served in a breezy russet setting in the higher reaches of the escalator. Don't get stuck on the sausages – there are lighter dishes like puff pastries. For dessert there are always *poffertjes* (Dutch pancakes) on the menu.
⊠ **17 Shelley St**
☎ **2838 9352**
e restaurant@orange
tree.com.hk Central
↖ ⊘ Sat-Sun noon-3pm, daily 6-10.30pm
V

Soho Soho
(6, C3) **$$$**
British
Post-colonially, New British food has taken off with Chuppies and Poms on expense accounts. It's creative (crumpet with smoked salmon), homy (roasted cod with new potatoes) and manly (chump of lamb with a pepper crust). Desserts are pure Brit treats like treacle tart and clotted cream.
⊠ **9 Old Bailey St**
☎ **2147 2618 e** soho@
hkdining.com Central
↖ ⊘ Mon-Sat noon-2.30pm, 7-10.30pm

Two Sardines
(6, D2) **$$$**
French
Independant French bistro which deserves the crowds it draws. The namesake fish comes grilled with a zesty sauce; the liver is worth trying too. The wine list leans predictably to the Gallic but is likely to please. Set lunches are excellent value.
⊠ **43 Elgin St** ☎ **2973 6618 e** sardines@
hk.super.net Central
↖ ⊘ Mon-Sat noon-3pm, 6.30pm-midnight

CAUSEWAY BAY

Chuen Cheung Kui
(5, G2) **$$**
Chinese, Hakka
Enlist a Cantonese dining companion or dive in bravely: there's not much English spoken here and the food is challenging. Gizzard soup and stomach tidbit are two of the less alluring menu items. The pulled chicken, a Hakka classic, is the dish to insist upon.
✉ 110-112 Percival St
☎ 2577 3833
Ⓜ Causeway Bay
🕐 11am-midnight

Cova Ristorante
(5, G3) **$$$**
Italian
This is as romantic as it gets in the basement of an office block: pastels, twinkling waiters and upholstered chairs. Whether it's pasta or pastries (lovely fruit tarts), charge up on a very good approximation of Milan's best coffee before you head back into the throng. There's nowhere to sit in the Prince's Bldg outlet: stand at the counter and slam it down.
✉ Shop B01, Lee Gardens, 33 Hysan Ave (also Shop 134, Prince's Bldg, Central; Shop 301, Pacific Place, Admiralty) ☎ 2907 3399 Ⓜ Causeway Bay 🚇 🕐 8.30am-11pm (high tea: 3-6pm)

Dining Area
(5, F3) **$$$**
International
Super groover hang-out with beautifully presented Euro-Canto food. There's freaky stuff going down in the kitchen: it's the kind of place where you might get wasabi in your focaccia and artichokes with your fried noodles. Never mind – it all tastes fine and everyone looks like a pop-star.
✉ 17 Lan Fong St
☎ 2915 0260 Ⓜ Causeway Bay 🕐 11.30am-11pm 🕭 yes **V**

eCafe
(5, F3) **$**
International
Sandwich and shake hang-spot with the cred of having underground radio webcast from an on-site booth (www.radiorepublic .com). Set lunches are around $35, dinners are under $60, or come between meals for coffee, cakes and snacks. Walk past the Extravaganza accessory shop to get inside.
✉ Shop F16, Fashion Island, 19 Great George St ☎ 2915 0040
Ⓜ Causeway Bay
🕐 noon-10.30pm
🕭 yes **V**

Forever Green
(5, G3) **$$**
Korean
Forever Green is the best place in town for Taiwanese food. Try traditional specialities such as oyster omelette, fried bean curd and *sanbeiji* (three-cup chicken). Noodle dishes are good value but other prices are fairly high. There's a pictorial menu to help out novices.
✉ 93-95a Leighton Rd (enter from Sun Wui Rd) ☎ 2890 3448
Ⓜ Causeway Bay
🕐 noon-3pm, 6pm-5am (Sun till 4am)
🕭 yes **V**

Genroku Sushi
(5, G2) **$$**
Japanese
Genroku is Hong Kong's most exotic fast-food chain. The sushi is very cheap and is served on a conveyor belt. The only drawback is the potentially long wait for seats,

---

Late-Night Bites

Most restaurants stop serving meals around 11pm but some won't let the chefs home till the wee hours. **Tai Woo Seafood Restaurant** (5, F2; ☎ 2893 0822; $$), 27 Percival St, Causeway Bay, is also known for its vegetarian dishes (try the bean curd with vegetarian crab roe). It's open till 3am. There's another branch at 14-16 Hillwood Rd, Tsim Sha Tsui (3, E5; ☎ 2730 8813).

Lan Kwai Fong is a logical place for late-night meals: **Benissimo** (6, D4; ☎ 2845 5533; $$$), 50 D'Aguilar St, has a special antipasti and pasta menu from 11.30pm to whenever. See also **369 Shanghai** (p. 82) and **Forever Green** (at right).

John May

especially during the 1-2pm lunch hour.
✉ Cnr Matheson St & Sharp St East ☎ 2889 8889 Ⓜ Causeway Bay ⏲ 11.30am-2am ♿ yes

Hello Kitty Café
(5, E3) $
Japanese, snacks
Cute food like toasties, waffles and sundaes along with more substantial Japanese soup noodles and dumplings. The decor is pink, the waitresses wear sparkly eyeshadow and the sliced pork comes with an eerie Hello Kitty stencil. Great choice for kids ('children set' $38).
✉ Shop 11, Chee On Bldg, 24 East Point Rd ☎ 2890 9021 Ⓜ Causeway Bay ⏲ 10am-11pm ♿ excellent V

Heng Fa Low
(5, F2) $
Chinese
This dessert hotspot has been in the neighbourhood for half a century. People crowd in here till late at night filling up on fruit and jelly concoctions. They tell us that *hasma* is frog's sperm soup – we dare you to call their bluff. There's a small selection of savoury dishes too.
✉ Po Ming Bldg, 49-57 Lee Garden Rd ☎ 2915 7797 Ⓜ Causeway Bay ⏲ 11am-midnight V

Paper Moon
(5, E4) $$
American
A garish good-time restaurant with massive portions of supposedly American food, well-intentioned but often missing the mark. There's usually live music in the evening.

✉ 8 Kingston St ☎ 2881 5070 Ⓜ Causeway Bay ⏲ 11.30am-1am (Fri-Sat till 2am, Sun till midnight) ♿ excellent V

Queen's Cafe
(5, G3) $$
Russian
This smallish Russian cafe has been here since 1952, accounting for its subdued yet assured atmosphere. The borsch and meat sets are pretty good. Head for nearby **Queen's Cake Shop** (15 Pak Sha Rd) for post-meal cakes and buns.
✉ Eton Tower, 8 Hysan Ave ☎ 2576 2658 Ⓜ Causeway Bay ⏲ noon-10pm

Peter piper eats here

Red Pepper
(5, F3) $$$
Chinese, Sichuanese
If you want to set your palate aflame, try this long-established restaurant's Sichuanese-style sliced pork in chilli sauce, accompanied by *dan dan min* (noodles in a spicy peanut soup). Also good are the deep-fried beans and sizzling prawns. This is a friendly place and the staff can help you order a meal to suit your taste.
✉ 7 Lan Fong Rd ☎ 2577 3811 Ⓜ Causeway Bay ⏲ 11.30am-midnight

The Stonegrill
(5, G3) $$$
International
Don't complain when your food arrives half-cooked – it's supposed to. Steak or fish arrives sunny-side up and sizzling on a slab of stone; you turn it over to taste. Local celebs have fallen big time for this half-baked idea: it's one of the trendiest restaurants in town. Book ahead.
✉ 1 Hoi Ping Rd (also Shop G319, Harbour City, Tsim Sha Tsui) ☎ 2576 1331 Ⓜ Causeway Bay ⏲ noon-3pm, 6.30pm-1am

Suikenkan
(4, F14) $$$
Japanese
Bar and restaurant with a nifty Samurai theme and an early evening happy hour that sees many drinkers turn into diners after the 3rd or 4th 'bottoms up'. This is a great place to snack and sip; there's a spiffing vego range.
✉ Kingstown Mansion, 313-323 Jaffe Rd ☎ 2573 1308 Ⓜ Causeway Bay ⏲ noon-1am V

Tack Hsin Restaurant
(5, F4) $$$
Chinese
Massive restaurant occupied by loud-talking families plunging food into sizzling hotpots. Beware of the prawns: they arrive alive and squirming on skewers. The English menu is limited – the deluxe hot-pot is a good bet. For breakfast there's pretty good dim sum.
✉ 1-13 Sugar St ☎ 2894 8899 Ⓜ Causeway Bay ⏲ 7am-1am ♿ yes

MONG KOK

Good Hope Noodle
(2, B2) **$**
Chinese, noodles
This busy noodle-stop is known far and wide for its wonton soups and shredded pork noodles with spicy bean sauce (ask for *tsa tseung)*. Good Hope is an eat-and-go sort of place – don't come here if you feel like slurping slowly and lingering.
✉ **146 Sai Yeung Choi St Sth (sth of Mong Kok Rd; see p. 48)** ☎ **2394 5967** Ⓜ **Mong Kok** ⏲ noon-1am ⚤ yes

Saint's Alp Teahouse
(2, B2) **$**
Snacks, Taiwanese
One in a chain of clean, cheap snackeries in Hong Kong – (look for the footprint sign). They're a great pit stop for Taiwanese-style frothy tea with tapioca drops and Chinese snacks like toast with condensed milk, shrimp balls, noodles and rice puddings.
✉ **61a Shantung St (see p. 48)** ☎ **2782 1438** Ⓜ **Mong Kok** ⏲ Sun-Thurs 10am-11pm, Fri-Sat 10am-midnight ⚤ yes **V**

Fruity fare, Mong Kok

NEW TERRITORIES

Cafe Aficionado
(1, E2) **$$$**
International
If you've got time to kill at the airport, this large cafeteria/restaurant is a good option. There are buffets for breakfast and lunch as well as a big all-day menu of Eastern and Western snacks and meals. The burgers are fantastic. Don't bother walking round to admire the art: it's on conveyer belts and it comes to you.
✉ **Regal Airport Hotel, 9 Cheong Tat Rd, Lantau Is** ☎ **2286 8888 (ext 6238)** Ⓜ **Airport** ⏲ 6am-1am ⚤ yes **V**

Chuen Kee Seafood Restaurant
(1, D8) **$$$$**
Chinese, Cantonese, seafood
See that queue of fidgety plastic basins which ends at the kitchen? That's dinner. Start by choosing your live seafood from the stall outside, tell the waiters how you want it cooked and then wait for it to progress, flipping and flapping to the kitchen. Most people eating at this no-frills restaurant order their catch steamed and simple.
✉ **51-55 Hoi Pong St (on the waterfront), Sai Kung** ☎ **2791 1195; 2792 9294** Ⓜ **Choi Hung (then bus 92 or minibus 1, 1a, 4)** ⏲ 11am-11pm ⚤ yes

Federal Restaurant
(2, B3) **$$**
Chinese, Cantonese, dim sum
Bustling restaurant, (not Federal Seafood),so big that the waiters have walkie-talkies. Yum cha is served until mid-afternoon and Cantonese a la carte at dinner. The yum cha menu is only in Chinese – ask your waiter to choose for you or stickybeak at other tables and point.

Feature windows look onto a very Hong Kong vista of apartments; the MTR station is right downstairs.
✉ **3rd fl, Hollywood Plaza, 3 Lung Poon St, Diamond Hill** ☎ **2626 0011** Ⓜ **Diamond Hill** ⏲ 7.30am-11pm ⚤ yes

Jaspa's
(1, D8) **$$$**
European
Multi-ethnic Jaspa's in Sai Kung attracts expats who can't face another round with chopsticks and trendy locals dining on pasta, stir-fries and steaks; there's an excellent vegetarian selection. The atmosphere is rollicking Mediterranean.
✉ **13 Sha Tsui Path (opp. the playground), Sai Kung** ☎ **2792 6388** ✉ **pasta@asiaonline .net** Ⓜ **Choi Hung (then bus 92 or minibus 1, 1a, 4)** ⏲ 10am-10.30pm (Sun from 9.30am) ⚤ yes **V**

SHEUNG WAN

Korea Garden
(4, C3) $$$
Korean
This comfortable restaurant serves a delicious array of appetisers (dried fish, salad, pickles, chillied cabbage leaves, spring rolls) which come as side dishes to BBQ dishes (sizzled at your table), kimchi (wouldn't be Korean without it) pancakes, grilled fish and ground meat in egg batter.
✉ **Blissful Bldg, 247 Des Voeux Rd Central** ☎ **2542 2339; 2854 3501** Ⓜ **Sheung Wan** 🚢 **Macau Ferry** ⏱ **11am-3am** **V**

Leung Hing Seafood Restaurant
(4, C1) $$
Chinese, Chiu Chow
The Chiu Chow region's main cooking ingredients – seafood, goose and duck – are extensively employed and delectably prepared. Try the classic sliced goose (cold) and soya in vinegar, and then revel in the lip-smacking desserts.
✉ **32 Bonham Strand West** ☎ **2850 6666** Ⓜ **Sheung Wan** ⏱ **noon-2am**

SOUTHERN HONG KONG ISLAND

The Boathouse
(2, E4) $$$
International
Previously a theme restaurant (this explains the Gothic cutlery and skull table legs), things are a lot sunnier here these days. Salads, bruschetta and Med-inspired mains make up the bulk of the Boathouse's fleet. Aim for sea views. Spinnaker's Bar downstairs serves snacks all day.
✉ **86-88 Stanley Main St** ☎ **2813 4467** 🚌 **6, 6a, 6x, 260x** ⏱ **10.30am-midnight** **V**

Jumbo Floating Restaurant
(2, D2) $$$
Chinese
Floating restaurants have made Aberdeen world famous. Jumbo's interior looks like Beijing's Imperial Palace crossbred with a Las Vegas casino. It's not so much a restaurant as an institution. That's how diners should view it, since the food often leaves something to be desired. Transport to and from the restaurants is via boats, which run between piers at the Aberdeen Promenade and next to the Aberdeen Marina Club.
✉ **Aberdeen Marina** ☎ **2873 7111** 🚢 **Aberdeen** 🚌 **70, 75** ⏱ **Mon-Sat 11am-11.30pm, Sun 7am-11pm**

Lucy's
(2, E4) $$$
Continental
Easy-going place that doesn't overwhelm with choice but with just how good the food is. The menu changes frequently as fresh produce and inspiration strikes, but the offerings tend to honest fusion rather than fancy flim-flammery. There's a good selection of wines by the glass.
✉ **64 Stanley Main St** ☎ **2813 9055** 🚌 **6, 6a, 6x, 260x** ⏱ **noon-3pm, 7-10pm** **V**

Tables 88
(2, E4) $$$
International
Tables 88 is housed in what used to be the local police station. The building's history is put to good use: a dungeon-like holding cell is now a private dining room. The food is continental with pan-Oriental flourishes and the occasional wry twist ('pork chops marinated in secrecy').
✉ **88 Stanley Village Rd** ☎ **2813 6262** 🚌 **6, 6a, 6x, 260x** ⏱ **11.30am-10.30pm**

The Verandah
(2, D3) $$$$
Continental, Asian
In the new-colonial bit of the wavy Repulse Bay condos, The Verandah is hushed and formal with heavy white tablecloths and demurely clinking cutlery. The brunch is famous (book way ahead and dream about the caviar-topped eggs benedict); the afternoon tea is the south side's best.
✉ **The Repulse Bay, 109 Repulse Bay Rd** ☎ **2812 2722** 🚌 **61** ⏱ **10am-10.30pm (afternoon tea 3-5.30pm)**

Jumpin' jumbo junks

Welcome Garden
(2, D5) $$
Cantonese
Breezy restaurant with an outdoor patio near sparkling Shek O Beach. The menu is like an extensive family album full of snapshots of favoured meals. Its deep-fried chicken is recommended (the chooks are fresh-killed). The fried milk is worth trying too. (The Thai place opposite has lots of loyal fans as well).
✉ 770 Shek O Village ☎ 2809 2836 🚇 Shau Kei Wan (then bus 9)
🕐 11.30am-10.30pm V

Meat-Free Dining

It can be hard to keep to a strict vegetarian diet in Hong Kong's Chinese restaurants. Most broths are meaty and chefs often see no harm in using oyster sauce and chicken stock in apparently safe vegetable dishes. There are some specialist Chinese vegetarian restaurants though. See **Fat Heung Lam** (p. 70), **Joyful Vegetarian** (p. 83) and **Miu Gute Cheong** (p. 83).

Other places with good awareness of vegetarian's needs are **Eating Plus** (p. 70), **Mughal Room** (p. 71), **M at the Fringe** (p. 72) and **Le Rendez-vous** (p. 73).

TSIM SHA TSUI

A Touch of Spice
(3, F6) $$
Indonesian, Vietnamese
One of four trendy restaurant/bars stacked up at 10 Knutsford Terrace. This one does Indo-Viet curries, noodles and fry-ups. It's all pretty cheap unless you go for the seafood – if you do want fish, you might rather try **Island Seafood** on the ground floor.
✉ 10 Knutsford Tce ☎ 2312 1118 e customerserv@kingparrot.com 🚇 Tsim Sha Tsui/Jordan 🕐 noon-3pm, 6-11pm V

Café Beaubourg
(3, F6) $$
French
This cute and narrow nook is tucked away in a street full of wedding gear shops. Pull up a pew for reasonable coffee, croquemonsieur and madame (the lady comes with an egg) and crepes both sweet and savoury. Hearty pastas are also available.
✉ Shop B, 58-60a

Kimberley Rd ☎ 2721 2939 🚇 Tsim Sha Tsui 🕐 11am-11pm ♿ yes V

Chinese Restaurant
(3, H4) $$$$
Chinese
It may not win any awards for its name, but the Chinese Restaurant has a solid reputation for its seasonal menu and its dim sum. If you order the Peking duck you'll get a numbered certificate, linking you to the bird forever. Solo diners will appreciate the set menu for one.
✉ Hyatt Regency Hotel, 67 Nathan Rd ☎ 2311 1234 (ext 2881) 🚇 Tsim Sha Tsui ⛴ Star Ferry 🕐 11.30am-3pm (Sun from 10.30am), 6.30-11pm ♿ yes V

El Cid
(3, F6) $$
Spanish
El Cid does justice to Spanish classics such as paella, and has an excellent assortment of tapas.

Also on hand is a healthy selection of imported wine. It's a congenial place with red and white checked tablecloths and an easy-splash tiled floor. It's as popular with locals as it is with expats.
✉ 12-14 Knutsford Tce ☎ 2312 1898 🚇 Tsim Sha Tsui/Jordan 🕐 noon-2.30pm, 6pm-midnight (wine bar serves tapas until 1am) ♿ yes V

Felix
(3, J5) $$$$
International
Felix has a fantastic setting, both inside and out. You're sure to pay as much attention to the views and the Philippe Starck interior as the food. Towering ceilings and hulking copperclad columns surround the Art Deco tables. Even the view from the urinal is dizzying. The food is dainty, sometimes sublime, fusion (think lobster nachos).
✉ The Peninsula ☎ 2920 2888 (ext 3188)

🚇 Tsim Sha Tsui
⛴ Star Ferry ⏰ 6pm-2am ♿ no **V**

Gaddi's
(3, J5) $$$$
French
Gaddi's maintains its reputation as the premier French restaurant in Hong Kong. It's boasted virtually the same menu (and some of the same staff) for 30 years. This is the sort of place where your grapes arrive peeled and sauces are routinely swirled with truffles or caviar. Romantic diners may enjoy one of the main courses served for two.
✉ The Peninsula
☎ 2920 2888 (ext 3171) 🚇 Tsim Sha Tsui ⏰ noon-2.30pm, 7-11pm ♿ no

Gaylord
(3, H4) $$$
Indian, vegetarian
Venerable Gaylord has been going strong since 1972. Dim lighting, booth seating and live Indian music usher you into a cosy world of spicy dining. You will hardly be able to tear yourself away from the remains of chicken tikka and

pappadam crumbs and return to the real world. There's a great lunch buffet.
✉ 23-25 Ashley Rd
☎ 2376 1001 🚇 Tsim Sha Tsui ⛴ Star Ferry ⏰ noon-3pm, 6-11pm ♿ yes **V**

Many happy noodles

Happy Garden Noodle & Congee Kitchen
(3, G3) $
Chinese, Cantonese
The Happy Garden cooks up some of Kowloon's best noodles and congee. It's a little more expensive than some of the backstreet joints but it's a heap more elegant and there's an English menu for those who are sick of pointing

and pot luck.
✉ 76 Canton Rd
☎ 2377 2604 🚇 Tsim Sha Tsui ⛴ Star Ferry ⏰ 7am-12.30am ♿ yes **V**

Lai Ching Heen
(3, K6) $$$$
Chinese, Cantonese
Don't let the elegant interior and stunning view distract you from exquisite Cantonese food that excites the palate while bowing deeply to tradition. Scallops are matched with pear, duck with kiwi, and anything on the menu can be paired with an appropriate wine. The menu changes with each lunar month, and if the selections get confusing, there's always a waiter hovering nearby to answer questions.
✉ Regent Hotel, 18 Salisbury Rd ☎ 2721 1211 (ext 2243) 🚇 Tsim Sha Tsui ⏰ noon-2.30pm, 6-11pm

Peking Restaurant
(3, D4) $$
Chinese, Peking
This no-frills restaurant keeps Peking duck fans merrily chomping away. If

Kid-Friendly Kitchens
Children are generally welcome in Hong Kong's restaurants – we've indicated the few restaurants that aren't cool for kids, as well as the ones that are particularly family friendly (look for the '♿' in reviews). Hardly any restaurants have highchairs or booster seats so bring your own if you can't do without. Though most restaurants don't do special children's serves, Chinese food lends itself to sharing and it's easy to create your own munchkin-sized portions.

The **Restaurant Marché** in the Peak Tower (p. 81) is super kid-friendly, with a play area and a children's menu. In Causeway Bay, **Paper Moon** (p. 75) has American food and a kids' menu.

duck doesn't do it for you, try the Peking-style crab dishes and pastries.

✉ 227 Nathan Rd
☎ 2730 1315
Ⓜ Jordan
🕐 11am-10.30pm

Restaurant Osaka
(3, H4) **$$**

Japanese

A splash of class above the hustle of Ashley Rd, this atmospheric restaurant has pinafored waitresses and a menu which extends from sushi to steaks via hotpots. There are reasonably priced set lunches.

✉ 14 Ashley Rd
☎ 2376 3323 Ⓜ Tsim Sha Tsui 🕐 noon-3pm, 6-11pm **V**

Salisbury Dining Room
(3, J4) **$$$**

International, buffet

Unlimited sushi and smoked salmon make the Salisbury buffets a pretty good bet. Book ahead if you want a table by the window and unimpeded harbour views. Guzzlers will be glad to note that the buffets include bottomless wine and draught beer.

✉ YMCA, 41 Salisbury Rd ☎ 2268 7000
Ⓜ Tsim Sha Tsui
🚢 Star Ferry 🕐 Mon-Sat noon-2.30pm, daily 6.15-9.30pm ♿ yes **V**

Spring Deer
(3, H6) **$$$**

Chinese

Spring Deer, hidden up a smelly staircase in a nondescript building, serves some of the crispiest Peking duck in town. The food isn't cheap but you can be sure you're not paying extra for atmosphere: obviously no money has been spent on

Kowloon City

The area behind the old Kai Tak airport is a vibrant local neighbourhood with herbalists, jewellers, tea merchants, bird shops and lots of restaurants. This part of town is famous for its Thai restaurants. Try **Thai Farm Restaurant** (2, A3; ☎ 2382 0992; $$), 21-23 Nam Kok Rd, for green curry pork and spicy prawn soup.

There are a bunch of Cantonese restaurants along Fuk Lo Tsun Rd, including **Cannes Restaurant** (2, A3; ☎ 2382 7333; $$) at No 37, where you can get fresh seafood. **Tenka Bakery** (2, A3; ☎ 2781 2789; $) at No 11 is an unostentatious place for fluffy buns, sausage rolls and sunshiney custard tarts. Over the road at No 12 is a **snake shop** which sells bowls of snake soup for $23. Take buses 1, 1a, 5, 5c from Tsim Sha Tsui to get to Kowloon City.

the decor for a couple of decades. The Deer is extremely popular, so book in advance.

✉ 42 Mody Rd
☎ 2366 4012 Ⓜ Tsim Sha Tsui 🚢 Star Ferry
🕐 noon-2.30pm, 6-11pm

Spring Moon
(3, J5) **$$$**

Chinese, Cantonese

Inside the grand Peninsula, Spring Moon is a most impressive restaurant. Complementing the high standards of the hotel, the Cantonese food is excellently prepared, and the ambience is stunning.

✉ The Peninsula
☎ 2315 3160 Ⓜ Tsim Sha Tsui 🕐 11.30am-4.30pm (Sun from 11am), 6-10.30pm

Valentino
(3, H6) **$$$**

Italian

Romantic Italian classic with soft lights and nuzzling music nightly. The seasonal menu has super soups (look out for a light tomato and

zucchini broth in summer) and a good range of salads, pasta and meats.

✉ Ocean View Court, 27a Chatham Rd Sth
☎ 2721 6449 Ⓜ Tsim Sha Tsui 🚢 HKF Hoverferry 🚌 5c, 8
🕐 noon-11pm **V**

Wan Loong Court
(3, J4) **$$$**

Chinese, Cantonese

Wonderful Cantonese food with deft modern touches: the dim sum here takes some beating. Standout dumplings include steamed beef with tangerine peel and fish with lemongrass and minced squid. The house special dessert is tai chi cake, a chestnut paste and poppy seed pastry. The menu, including the specials, is translated into English and service is great.

✉ Kowloon Hotel, 19-21 Nathan Rd ☎ 2734 3722 Ⓔ khh@peninsula.com Ⓜ Tsim Sha Tsui 🚢 Star Ferry
🕐 Mon-Fri 11am-3pm, 6-11.30pm, Sat-Sun 11am-11.30pm **V**

TSIM SHA TSUI EAST

Fruit Stop
(3, G7) $
Chinese
Student hang-out with a jazz soundtrack and a battalion of shiny young folk on deck. The decor is plastic but the food is healthy. Crunch on cornflakes, fresh fruit and vegetable juices and a wacky selection of sandwiches (how's banana and cinnamon? not weird enough? try strawberry yoghurt on toast). There are noodles too, if you want to keep it Asian.
✉ **Toyo Mall, 94 Granville Rd (also Shop G119, Harbour City)** ☎ **2973 6873** ⊕ **Tsim Sha Tsui** 🚇 **HKF Hoverferry** 🚌 **5c, 8** ◷ **Mon-Sat 7.30am-10.30pm, Sun noon-10.30pm** ♿ **yes** **V**

Sabatini
(3, G7) $$$
Italian
Classy Sabatini is a direct copy of its namesake in Rome, with designs painted on the walls and ceilings, and a polished tile floor. Even classic Italian dishes, such as fettuccine carbonara, come across as light in the best sense, leaving room to sample the exquisite desserts. The wine list is also excellent.
✉ **Royal Garden Hotel, 69 Mody Rd** ☎ **2733 2000** ⊕ **Tsim Sha Tsui** 🚇 **HKF Hoverferry** ◷ **noon-2.30pm, 6-11pm**

VICTORIA PEAK

Cafe Deco
(4, K2) $$$
International
The philosophy seems to be that views, live jazz and buzzy ambience are enough to keep the punters happy. And if you stick to cocktails and simple fresh food (the oyster bar, the sushi) you won't go too wrong. But the more artistry the food attempts, the more it falls down.
✉ **Peak Galleria, 118 Peak Rd** ☎ **2849 5111** **e** **sales@peakcafe.com** 🚌 **15 (from Exchange Sq), minibus 1 (from Star Ferry)** 🚋 **Peak Tram** ◷ **Sun-Thurs 10am-midnight, Fri-Sat 10am-1am (kitchen closes 11.30pm)** **V**

Peak Café
(4, K2) $$$
International
East meets west at the Peak. The food is always delicious, and includes Chinese, Indian, Thai and some Western dishes (the Indian food is usually the best bet). What really makes this place is the amazing setting: a vaulted ceiling, elegant decor and one of Hong Kong's finest bars. There's a large outdoor terrace which is very romantic on a warm evening.
✉ **121 Peak Rd** ☎ **2849 7868** **e** **peakcafe@ peakcafe.com** 🚌 🚋 **see Cafe Deco** ◷ **10.30am-midnight (kitchen closes 10.45pm)** **V**

Restaurant Marché
(4, K2) $$
International
Wander over and order from hawker market-style kitchenettes offering roasts, curries, grills, pasta, sushi and more. Buffet specials are available at lunch and from around 10pm. There are several different eating areas, most of them with spectacular views from the Peak Tower. This is a great place to bring kids: there's a play area and lots of child-friendly food.
✉ **L6 & 7, Peak Tower, 128 Peak Rd (enter from L4)** ☎ **2849 2000** 🚌 🚋 **see Cafe Deco** ◷ **10.30am-midnight (kitchen closes 10.45pm)** ♿ **excellent** **V**

Fill up at the Peak Café then walk it off on the Peak.

Hong Kong Tourist Association

WAN CHAI

369 Shanghai Restaurant
(4, F12) **$$**
Chinese, Shanghainese
Low-key Shanghai food that's nothing like five-star but does the dumpling job. It's family-run and there are some good comfy booths in the window. It's open late too, so you can come here after a draining dance.
✉ 30-32 O'Brien Rd
☎ 2527 2343 ⊕ Wan Chai ⊙ noon-4am
♿ yes

American Restaurant
(4, G11) **$$**
Chinese
Don't be put off by the name, or by the grimy appearance. The friendly American has been serving excellent Peking cuisine for over 50 years. Most of its customers are regulars. As you'd hope, the Peking duck and the beggar's chicken (order in advance) are very good.
✉ Goldenstar Bldg, 20 Lockhart Rd ☎ 2527 1000 ⊕ Wan Chai
⊙ 11am-11.30pm ♿ yes

Carrianna Chiu Chow Restaurant
(4, F14) **$$$**
Chinese, Chiu Chow
For Chiu Chow food, the Carrianna rates right up there. Try the cold dishes (goose slices and cold crab), pork with tofu or chicken with chin jew sauce. The place is usually crowded, but there are plenty of tables.
✉ AXA Centre, 151 Gloucester Rd (enter from Tonnochy Rd)
☎ 2511 1282 ⊕ Wan Chai ⊙ 11am-midnight
♿ yes

How do you like your eggs: over-easy or 1000 year old?

Cinta
(4, G11) **$$**
Filipino, Indonesian, Malaysian
A friendly restaurant and lounge with a big South-East Asian menu that runs from rotis to laksas to gado gado and back again. There's live music every night.
✉ Shing Yip Bldg, 10 Fenwick St ☎ 2527 1199 ⊕ Wan Chai
⊙ 11am-3pm, 6pm-2am ♿ yes **V**

Dynasty
(4, E12) **$$$**
Chinese, Cantonese
Stylish Cantonese restaurant that does a much-lauded daily dim sum. This is a good choice for business lunches: the atmosphere is refined, being more hum and hush than the normal dim sum clatter. If you're ordering from the menu, try the shredded beef in yakiniku sauce.
✉ Renaissance Harbour View Hotel, 1 Harbour Rd ☎ 2802 8888 (ext 6971) ⊕ Wan Chai
⊙ noon-2.30pm, 6.30-10.30pm (Sun from 11.30am)

Fook Lam Moon
(4, G11) **$$$$**
Chinese
Long known as one of

Hong Kong's top Cantonese restaurants, Fook Lam Moon makes sure you're taken care of from the minute you walk in the door. Seafood is the speciality: the shark's fin soup is among the best in town. Try the house speciality pan-fried lobster balls too.
✉ 35-45 Johnston Rd (also at Luna Court, 53-59 Kimberley Rd, Tsim Sha Tsui) ☎ 2866 0663 ⊕ Wan Chai
⊙ 11.30am-3pm, 6.30-11.30pm ♿ yes

Harry Ramsden's
(4, H12) **$$**
British, seafood
For fish and chips, nowhere comes close Harry's. Brits trip over each other to get a slab of haddock and a fistful of greasies. The service is a bit slow and sloppy, but the fish is excellent and bargain-priced: $98 gets you a meal and drink pack.
✉ Shop 3-4, Wu Chung House, 213 Queen's Rd East ☎ 2832 9626
e harryshk@hkabc.net ⊕ Wan Chai
⊙ 11.30am-11pm
♿ yes **V**

Open Kitchen
(4, F11) **$$**
International
When your cafeteria serves

up delicious stuffed eggplant to go with a gorgeous harbour view, you know you're probably on the right track. Open Kitchen is a good, cheapish, arty option for meals, snacks or drinks at the bar. Bring your ticket stub from the cinema downstairs to get a free drink with your meal.

✉ **Hong Kong Arts Centre, 2 Harbour Rd** ☎ 2827 2923 e information@open kitchen.com 🅗 Wan Chai ⏰ 11am-11pm ♿ yes Ⓥ

Port Cafe
(4, D12) $$$
International
Come for a satisfying bite between sessions or a quiet getaway when the convention centre isn't busy. The Port is sophisticated yet relaxed, and serves fine Euro/Italian cuisine, high tea and a Sunday BBQ buffet. You're jutting out into the harbour so the views are stunning. Note that it's not open for dinner.
✉ **Convention & Exhibition Centre, 1 Expo Dr** ☎ 2582 7731 🅗 Wan Chai 🚟 Star

Ferry ⏰ Mon-Sat 11am-6pm, Sun noon-6pm Ⓥ

Steam and Stew Inn
(4, H11) $$
Chinese
The Inn serves 'home-style' Cantonese food – steamed, stewed or boiled. Try the steamed mushroom stuffed with minced pork and crab-meat sauce. It's popular, so consider booking ahead.
✉ **Hing Wong Court, 21-23 Tai Wong St East** ☎ 2529 3913 🅗 Wan Chai ⏰ 11.30am-2.30pm, 5.30-11.30pm

YAU MA TEI

Bali Restaurant
(3, C5) $$
Indonesian
The food is pretty good and the service is friendly but the best thing about Bali Restaurant is its superb tackiness: a permanent 'happy birthday' sign, vinyl booths separated by fake brick walls and a 'resort'-style bar. Try the yellow rice special dish (pictured on the Chinese menu) and the pork satays.
✉ **10 Nanking St (off Nathan Rd)** ☎ 2780 2902 🅗 Jordan ⏰ noon-11pm ♿ yes

Hing Kee
(3, A4) $
Chinese
There's only one dish served at this semi-outdoor stall: rice cooked over charcoal in an earthenware pot and topped with either beef or chicken. It's a traditional winter dish but there are enough rice fans to keep the stall in business all year.
✉ **19 Temple St (enter from Hi Lung Lane)** ☎ 2384 3647 🅗 Yau

Ma Tei ⏰ 5.30pm-midnight ♿ yes

Joyful Vegetarian
(2, B2) $$
Vegetarian
This popular restaurant serves up great all-vegetarian meals. The vegetable country-style hotpot is made with a ravishing range of fungi. There's a snack stall out the front if you need a bite on the fly.
✉ **530 Nathan Rd (nth of Waterloo Rd; see p. 48)** ☎ 2780 2230 🅗 Yau Ma Tei ⏰ 11am-11pm ♿ yes Ⓥ

Miu Gute Cheong Vegetarian Restaurant
(3, C4) $
Chinese, vegetarian
Cheap, cheerful and family-oriented vegetarian restaurant. There's a bit of spill-over bustle from Temple St but an unruffled serenity prevails. The tofu is fresh and firm, the vegetables are the pick of the market and the tea flows freely.
✉ **31 Ning Po St (off Nathan Rd)** ☎ 2771 6217 🅗 Yau Ma Tei ⏰ 11am-11pm ♿ yes Ⓥ

Need Coffee?
Coffee in Hong Kong tends to be stewed to the max then mixed with sweetened condensed milk. You can get a decent espresso though. **The First Cup** (3, H4; ☎ 2316 7793), 3 Lock Rd, Tsim Sha Tsui, is a tiny caffeine dispensary. **? Coffee Shop** (6, C3; ☎ 2581 2128), 45 Cochrane St, Central, is a sandwich nook which does mean hot or iced coffees. Excellent coffee is can be had at **Cova** (p. 74). Bearable chain coffee is available from **Pacific Coffee Company** and **Delifrance** outlets in just about every shopping centre. There's a **Starbucks** (5, G3) in Causeway Bay.

Hoorah for Yum Cha!

Yum cha (literally 'to drink tea') is the usual way to refer to dim sum, the uniquely Cantonese snacks that are served for breakfast or lunch (usually between about 7am and 2pm). Eating dim sum is a social occasion, consisting of many separate dishes which are meant to be shared. The bigger your group the better!

Dim sum delicacies are normally steamed in a small bamboo basket. In most dim sum restaurants you order from a menu but in older-style places, the baskets are stacked up on pushcarts and rolled around the dining room. Just stop the waiter and choose something from the cart. Don't worry about trying everything you're offered: each pushcart has a different selection, so stagger your selections to give your stomach a fair go. It's estimated there are about 1000 dim sum dishes – you'd be doing very well to sample 10 in one sitting.

Dim sum restaurants can be so large that the servers use walkie-talkies to communicate with the kitchen. They get very crowded, especially at lunchtime and even more so on weekends. There's a friendly, fun buzz as the groups, often extended families, talk loudly and share food and tea.

The 10th floor of Times Square shopping centre in Causeway Bay holds a few restaurants doing a roaring trade. Choose between **Heichinrou** (5, G2; ☎ 2506 2333; $$), the most elegant place up here, **King Palace** (5, G2; ☎ 2506 3939; $$) and the phenomenally popular **Eminence** (5, G2; ☎ 2506 2188; $$), where you take a ticket and wait your turn. **KamBoat** (4, C3; ☎ 2815 7838; $$$), 2nd fl, Golden Centre, 188 Des Voeux Rd, Central, is known for its beautifully presented dim sum. **Luk Yu Tea House** (p. 71), **Lin Heung Tea House** (p. 73), **City Hall** (p. 70) and **Wan Loong Court** (p. 80) are also good for dim sum.

Dim sum dishes include:
chà sìu bàu – barbecued pork buns
chéung fán – steamed rice flour rolls with shrimp, beef or pork
chìng chàu sìchoi – fried green vegetable of the day
chùn gúen – fried spring rolls
fán gwó – steamed dumplings with pork, shrimp and bamboo shoots
fung jàu – fried chicken's feet
gàisì cháumìn – fried crispy noodles with shredded chicken
gòn sìu yìmin – dry-fried noodles
hà gáu – shrimp dumplings
ham sùi gok – fried rice flour triangles (usually with pork inside)
ho yip fan – rice wrapped in lotus leaf
pai gwàt – steamed spare ribs
sàn jùk ngau yok – steamed minced beef balls
sìu mai – pork and shrimp dumplings
woo gok – deep-fried taro puffs

entertainment

When you want to be wowed, Hong Kong is a capable entertainer. Most weeks, half a dozen local arts companies perform anything from Cantonese opera to an English-language version of a Chekhov play. Locally cultivated drama and dance is among the best in Asia, and the schedule of foreign performances is also often impressive – recent imports have included French equestrian opera, a franchise of *Riverdance* and a John Lill 'piano fest'. Luckily, the government subsidises the cost of international acts, so ticket prices can be very reasonable: around $50 for a seat up the back for a local performance and up to $300 for a top-class international act.

This isn't to say that Hong Kong is a cultural honey pot. Many government initiatives appear more motivated by the idea that Hong Kong *should* be an arty town, than by a heartfelt commitment to artistic endeavour. Art generally plays second fiddle to commerce, sometimes with a comic outcome – when residents complained about noise spillage from stadium concerts, suggested solutions included turning off the stage speakers and issuing concert-goers with headphones.

Information

The *South China Morning Post* has daily arts and entertainment reviews and listings and a Sunday liftout – most content is available online (www.totallyhk.com). Free local magazines, *HK* and *bc* are up on club nights, drinks deals and happy hours, as well as art exhibitions and performances. The HKTA has several free information publications, including the monthly *Official Hong Kong Guide* and the weekly *What's On*.

Bookings

Bookings for most cultural events can be made through URBTIX (☎ 2734 9009; 10am-8pm; see *HK* for outlets). Another concert and show booker is Ticket City (☎ 2805 2804; www.ticketcity-asia.com).

Top Spots

The biggest bar crawl is definitely **Lan Kwai Fong**, a narrow L-shaped alley in Central lined with nightspots. The clientele is upwardly mobile: ruddy expats mix with local business types and trendies. Nearby **Soho** has more of a restaurant scene and a number of bars have opened along the escalator route and its cross streets. The newest hang-out is **Boho** ('BelOw HOllywood Rd'), where some slick gay/straight bars and clubs have cropped up.

Wan Chai is sleaze territory, with awful hostess bars along Lockhart Rd and lots of zippy club action and late-night covers-band venues. It's the part of town that kicks on latest – handy if it's dawn and you still want to dance.

Kowloon is less happening. There are three basic clusters of bars in Tsim Sha Tsui: along Ashley Rd; within the triangle formed by Hanoi and Chatham Rds and Prat Ave; and up by Knutsford Tce. Tsim Sha Tsui East is swanky hostess-bar territory.

Hong Kong Tourist Association

A drink in a cool bar isn't the only heat-beater, try Ocean Park (p. 38).

SPECIAL EVENTS

late January/early February *Chinese New Year* – fireworks, flower fairs
Yuen Siu (Lantern Festival) – following New Year traditional lanterns are displayed throughout the city and paraded through the streets
Fringe Festival – eclectic performances sponsored by the Fringe Club

February *HK Arts Festival* – month-long series of performing arts events
Golf Open – at the Royal Hong Kong Golf Club
International Marathon – held in Sha Tin

March *Food Festival* – seasonal food fair with tastings and excursions

late March/early April *HK Rugby Sevens* – HK Rugby Sevens (this famous 3-day carnival is the city's biggest sporting event)
Hong Kong International Film Festival – a cinematic showcase from Hong Kong and the rest of the world

April/May *Tin Hau Festival* – celebrations on the water in honour of the patroness of fishing people

May *Cheung Chau Bun Festival* – three-day Taoist munch and march

June *Dragon Boat Festival* – boat races and fireworks

mid-July to late-August *International Arts Carnival* – focuses on the Cultural Centre with performances around town
mid-July *Hong Kong Fashion Week* – parades and events at the Convention & Exhibition Centre and at shopping centres around town.

mid-September *Mid-Autumn Festival* – romantic moon-watching celebration
late September/early October *International Cricket Series* – two-day event

October *Festival of Asian Arts* – one of Asia's major cultural events; biennial

November *HK Folk Festival* – international and local performers

December *Euro-Christmas* – turkey basting and tree decorating

Hong Kong Tourist Association

Wish upon a tree during Chinese New Year.

CLASSICAL ARTS & COMEDY

Charlie Luciano's

(4, F11) Cabaret venue with a penchant for comedy. If you don't want dinner and a show, you can stand at the bar and giggle from there. The artists are usually English, American or Canadian; the laughs are pretty mainstream.
✉ **13 Fenwick St, Wan Chai** ☎ **2529 6888**
e **info@charlie lucianos.com** 🚇 **Wan Chai** ⏰ **noon-3am (shows from around 8pm)** ⑤ **$200, $320 with dinner**

City Hall (4, E7)

Hosts classical recitals, Chinese music concerts and lots of dance. City Contemporary Dance Company is an exciting local outfit that performs here. Recent productions combined dance, striptease and video, and choreographers shared the billing with fashion designers.
✉ **Concert Hall, City Hall, 7 Edinburgh Pl, Central** ☎ **2921 2840; 2734 9009 (bookings)** 🚇 **Central** 🚢 **Star Ferry** ⑤ **$100-200**

Fringe Theatres

(6, E5) The two theatres here host eclectic local and international performances in both Cantonese and English. There's usually something worth seeing.
✉ **2 Lower Albert Rd, Lan Kwai Fong, Central** ☎ **2521 7251**
🚇 **Central** ⑤ **$50-200**

HK Cultural Centre

(3, K4) With three large theatres, this is Hong Kong's premier performance venue, with regular Chinese music and opera performances. It's also home to the HK Repertory Theatre, HK Philharmonic Orchestra, and major touring companies usually play here.
✉ **Cnr Salisbury & Canton Rds, Tsim Sha Tsui** ☎ **2734 2009**
🚇 **Tsim Sha Tsui** 🚢 **Star Ferry** ⑤ **$100-300**

HK Academy for Performing Arts

(4, F11) Stages local and overseas performances of dance, drama and music. The building was designed by local architect Simon Kwan. Right next door is the HK Arts Centre.
✉ **1 Gloucester Rd, Wan Chai** ☎ **2584 8500 (info); 2584 8514 (box office)** 🚇 **Wan Chai** 🚌 **10a, 20 or 21**

HK Arts Centre

(4, F11) This independent showcase for contemporary arts in all media emphasises home-grown talent. The theatre here hosts drama (often in English) by local companies such as the Hong Kong Players. See also *Pao Galleries* (p. 40) and *Lim Por Yen Theatre* (p. 88).
✉ **2 Harbour Rd, Wan Chai** ☎ **2582 0200**
🚇 **Wan Chai** 🚢 **Star Ferry** 🚌 **10a, 20, 21** ⑤ **$50-200**

Sunbeam Theatre

(2, C3) Cantonese opera can be seen here throughout the year. Performances generally run for about a week, and are usually held in the evening (sometimes there are matinees). The theatre is right above the MTR, on the north side of

Opera Outdoors

Cantonese opera is performed nightly at the corner of Temple St and Jordan Rd Nth (at the top of the night market) between 7 and 11pm. The 2nd Sunday of each month (2.30-5.30pm) sees **Harbourfront Fest** in the forecourt of the HK Cultural Centre. Performers range from acrobats to choirs.

Cantonese operatics

King's Rd, near the intersection with Shu Kuk St – look for the garish posters.
✉ **Kiu Fai Bldg, 423 King's Rd, North Point** ☎ **2563 2959** 🚇 **North Point** ⑤ **$50-300** ♿ **yes**

Viceroy (4, F14)

The Viceroy is the scene of one-off live bands, dance parties, salsa nights and the Punchline Comedy Club.
✉ **2nd fl, Sun Hung Kai Centre, 30 Harbour Rd, Wan Chai** ☎ **2827 7777** 🚇 **Wan Chai** ⏰ **noon-3pm, 6-11pm** ⑤ **shows $200-300**

CINEMAS

Most cinemas screen five sessions daily: 12.30, 2.30, 5.30, 7.30 and 9.30pm with extra 4 and 11.30pm screenings on weekends. Almost all Hong Kong films have English subtitles. Admission is usually $50 (half-price on Tuesday). You can book cinema tickets through Cityline (☎ 2317 6666).

Broadway Cinematheque

(3, A3) An unlikely place for an alternative cinema but it's worth coming up for new arthouse releases and rerun screenings. There's a cafe next door which serves good coffee and decent pre-flick food.
✉ **Prosperous Garden, 3 Public Sq St, Yau Ma Tei** ☎ **2322 9000** 🚇 **Yau Ma Tei** ☃ **yes**

Cine-Art House

(4, F14) This alternative cinema specialises in English-language flicks.
✉ **Sun Hung Kai Centre, 30 Harbour Rd, Wan Chai** ☎ **2827 4820** 🚇 **Wan Chai** ⛴ **Star Ferry** ⓢ **$50** ☃ **yes**

JP Cinema (5, E3)

There's no problem finding mainstream flicks in Causeway Bay. As well as JP's, there's a big UA complex in Times Square (☎ 2506 2822) right above the MTR. Be prepared for huge crowds on weekends.
✉ **JP Plaza, 22-36 Paterson St (cnr Great George St), Causeway Bay** ☎ **2881 5005** 🚇 **Causeway Bay** ☃ **yes**

Lim Por Yen Theatre

(4, F11) The Lim Por Yen is the place for classics, revivals, alternative screenings and travelling film festivals. The annual European Film Festival is usually held here in November.
✉ **HK Arts Centre, 2** Harbour Rd, Wan Chai ☎ **2582 0200 (reservations); 2582 0232 (information)** 🚇 **Wan Chai** ⓢ **$50** ☃ **yes**

Queen's Theatre

(4, E5) Queen's is one of the only movie houses in Central geared towards English-language films. It's a great old barn of a place and a very atmospheric spot to catch a film.
✉ **Luk Hoi Tung Bldg, 31 Queen's Rd (rear entrance), Central** ☎ **2522 7036** 🚇 **Central** ☃ **yes**

Silvercord Cinema

(3, G3) The easy-to-find Silvercord is right near the Star Ferry terminal. Its two

Up on the silver screen

theatres screen the latest Hollywood releases. Just up the road is the Ocean Theatre (☎ 2377 2100), Harbour City, 3 Canton Rd.
✉ **30 Canton Rd, Tsim Sha Tsui** ☎ **2388 3188** 🚇 **Tsim Sha Tsui** ⛴ **Star Ferry** ☃ **yes**

Hong Kong Films

Hong Kong is something of an 'Eastern Hollywood', churning out around 100 films each year, the third highest after Hollywood and India.

The new wave of Hong Kong films in the 1990s attracted fans worldwide, particularly with John Woo's blood-soaked epics *Hardboiled* and *The Killer*. John Woo has achieved international success with films such as *Face/Off* and *Mission Impossible 2*.

Hong Kong superstar Jackie Chan starred in *Rush Hour* while Lamma native, Chow Yun Fat, starred in *The Replacement Killers* and *Anna & the King*. Local actor Jet Li, of *Lethal Weapon 4* and *Romeo Must Die* fame, is another who has made good in Hollywood. Wong Kar-Wai, director of the cult hit *Chungking Express*, won the 1992 Palme d'Or at the Cannes Film Festival for his film *Happy Together* and Tony Leung Chiu Wai nabbed Best Actor at Cannes in 2000 for his role in Wong's *In the Mood For Love*.

UA Queensway

(4, G9) It's blessedly easy to sink your seat into the comfort offered by Hong Kong's plushest cinema. Its great sound system ensures you won't miss a whisper.

✉ **Pacific Place, 88 Queensway, Admiralty** ☎ 2869 0322 ⊕ Admiralty ♿ yes

Multicultural Offerings

International bodies who hold events in Hong Kong to promote their art and culture include:

British Council (4, G8; ☎ 2913 5125), 3 Supreme Court Rd, Admiralty

Alliance Française (4, G12; ☎ 2527 7825), 2nd fl, 123 Hennessy Rd, Wan Chai

Goethe Institut (4, F11; ☎ 2802 0088), 14th fl, HK Arts Centre, 2 Harbour Rd, Wan Chai

GAY & LESBIAN HONG KONG

The gay scene is clustered around Glenealy and Wyndham Sts, Central. There are one or two spots in Lan Kwai Fong, a couple in Boho, one in Sheung Wan and a string of clubs along Jaffe Rd, Wan Chai. See www.gaystation.com.hk for updated nightlife info.

Club 97 (6, D5)

A schmoozery which uses a selectively enforced 'members only' policy to turn away the badly dressed. There's a sceney gay happy hour on Fri nights, with free entry and half-price drinks. **Post 97**, the restaurant next door, has the same management.

✉ **Cosmos Bldg , 9-11 Lan Kwai Fong, Lan Kwai Fong, Central** ☎ 2586 1103 ⊕ Central ⏰ Mon-Fri 5pm-5am, Sat 10pm-5am, Sun 10pm-4am ⑤ $50-150

Home (6, C3)

A meet-n-greet for the beautiful people early, turning into a bump-n-grind later in the evening. This is one of the only places in Hong Kong that hosts 'girls who like girls' nights. Has karaoke on Monday eve.

✉ **2nd fl, 23 Hollywood Rd, Central** ☎ 9345 5858 ✉ atomicattack@ hotmail.com ⊕ Central

⏰ Mon-Fri 7pm-3am, Sat 10pm-6am ⑤ $100 on weekends

Petticoat Lane (6, C3)

Salon with a lightning bolt marble bar and young gentleman portraits on the walls. It's small, subdued and much more suited to chatting than bopping. There's a fair proportion of gay custom though it's popular with straights too.

✉ **2 Tun Wo Lane (off Cochrane St), Boho, Central** ☎ 2973 0642 ✉ petticoat@the97 group.com.hk ⊕ Central ⏰ Mon-Thurs 10am-2am, Fri-Sat 10am-3am, Sun 5pm-2am ⑤ free

Propaganda (6, C4)

As its ads are proud to proclaim, this is Hong Kong's premier gay meat market. There's no cover charge Mon-Wed, but charges creep up towards the weekend. Inside, there's a long undulating bar and plenty of mirrors so you can talent-spot.

✉ **1 Hollywood Rd**

(enter from Ezra Lane, off Cochrane St), Boho, Central ☎ 2868 1316 ⊕ Central ⏰ Mon-Thurs 9pm-2.30am, Fri-Sat 9pm-4am ⑤ $100+

Rice Bar (4, C3)

Rice is a small, vibey gay bar with a lounge area which sees a bit of dancing as it gets later. On-site tarot card and palm readers can help you out with life's important questions. If the answer is eating, there's cute food to be had on site.

✉ **33 Jervois St (cnr Mercer St), Sheung Wan** ☎ 2851 4800 ⊕ Sheung Wan ⏰ noon-2am ⑤ free

Zip Bar (4, F4)

Zip has gone to the splashy length of installing an outdoor waterfall and takes in most of Hong Kong Island's action. It gets very crowded on weekends.

✉ **2 Glenealy Rd, Central** ☎ 2523 3595 ⊕ Central ⏰ 6pm-2am ⑤ $100+

CLUBS & KARAOKE

The club scene is hot and vibed up. Cover charges ($50-200) sometimes include a drink or two and entrance can be free on particular theme nights.

Bahama Mama's Caribbean Bar

(3, F5) Bahama Mama's theme is tropical isle, complete with palm trees and surfboards. It's a friendly spot and stands apart from most of the other late-night watering holes. On Friday and Saturday nights there's a DJ spinning and folks out on the bonsai-sized dance floor.
✉ 4-5 Knutsford Tce, Tsim Sha Tsui ☎ 2368 2121 🚇 Tsim Sha Tsui/Jordan ⏰ Sun-Thurs 5pm-3am, Fri-Sat 5pm-4am ⑤ $100 after 11pm (Fri & Sat only)

Big Apple

(4, F12) The Big Apple is frequently nominated as one of Hong Kong's raunchiest nightspots. It's a hang-out for a young immigrant crowd hellbent on having a good time. Go and have a look at the great neon sign even if you're not up for a dance.
✉ 20 Luard Rd, Wan Chai ☎ 2529 3461 🚇 Wan Chai ⏰ Mon-Thurs 5pm-5am, Fri-Sun 2pm-5am ⑤ free ⚥ no

CE Top

(6, B3) This rooftop club is a stayer in Hong Kong's flighty club scene. Different nights feature a mix of house, trance, garage, soul and drum 'n' bass. Friday night's 'Club Elements' gets into hard house and breakbeats from 4am. Some nights have a strong gay leaning, but that's not to say it's not for straights.
✉ 3rd & 9th fl, 37-43 Cochrane St (enter behind the Dublin Jack bar), Central ☎ 2544 3584 🚇 Central ⏰ Tues-Fri 9pm-3am, Sat 9pm-4am ⑤ $100+

Club Bboss

(3, F8) The biggest, most garish hostess bar in town. It's a ridiculous scene: floor-shows, babes and men drinking cognac because they think it's classy.
✉ New Mandarin Plaza, 14 Science Museum Rd, Tsim Sha Tsui ☎ 2369 2883 🚇 Tsim Sha Tsui East ⚓ HKF Hoverferry ⏰ 1pm-4am ⑤ $460 day, $520 night

Club ing

(4, E12) Newly decked-out club with chatting lounges, a long bar, karaoke and disco. It's popular with a young Cantonese crowd. Dress smartly (no sandals, sneakers, tank tops). There's free entry and drinks for fashionable ladies on Thursday nights.
✉ L4, Renaissance Harbour View Hotel, 1 Harbour Rd, Wan Chai ☎ 2836 3690 🚇 Wan Chai ⚓ Star Ferry ⏰ 8pm-late ⑤ $100+

Club Temptation

(5, E2) Popular club with a strong line-up of DJs spinning house with a funky edge. This is one of the least trance-oriented clubs in Hong Kong. Women can bubble over with free champagne on Tuesday. Drinks specials contribute to a weekend party atmosphere.
✉ 4th & 9th fl, Kyoto Plaza, 491-499 Lockhart Rd, Causeway Bay ☎ 2833 5548 🚇 Causeway Bay ⏰ 5pm-4am ⑤ $150+

Energy Karaoke

(3, G5) New-fangled karaoke club with private booths: come with friends to choose from hundreds of songs in Chinese, Korean, Japanese and English and belt them out in your own padded cell. You can hear the warbling of wannabe popstars through the corridors.
✉ 8 Humphreys Ave (cnr Cameron St), Tsim

Raves

Hong Kong's most talked about dance parties are one-off raves, held in venues as diverse as the airport hotel and the Kwun Tong Ferry Pier. Raves are advertised in *HK*, www.gwylorecords.com, www.hkrave .com and in clubbing zines like *absolute* (they have it at HMV). Raves usually kick off around 11pm, push through to 7am and cost $200-400.

Richard Nebesky

Sha Tsui ☎ 2366 3388
🚇 Tsim Sha Tsui
🕐 noon-6am ⓢ free
for first 3 hrs if you
order drinks ⚥ yes

Joe Banana's (4, F12)
Signs advertise wet T-shirt
contests and welcome military personnel: there's the
tone. If you go with friends,
you can have some unre-
constructed fun.
Unaccompanied females
should expect a good sam-
pler of bad pick-up lines.
The bar has two-for-one
cocktails on Wednesday,
and a daily happy hour
(11.30am-10pm).
✉ Shiu Lam Bldg, 23
Luard Rd (cnr Jaffe Rd),
Wan Chai ☎ 2529
1811 ✉ jbmanagers@
joebananas.com
🚇 Wan Chai 🕐 Mon-
Thurs 11am-5am, Fri-
Sat 11am-6am, Sun
5pm-5am ⓢ $100 Fri &
Sat after 9pm (for men)
and 1am (for women)

The Jump (5, F2)
A neat and spacious
American-style bar and
restaurant with funky,
round booths and a menu
that starts with burgers
then runs south of the bor-
der to fajitas. The tight
dancefloor is usually hop-
ping on the weekend.
There's an all-you-can-drink
Sunday champagne brunch.
✉ 7th fl, Causeway
Bay Plaza Two, 463
Lockhart Rd, Causeway
Bay ☎ 2832 9007
🚇 Causeway Bay
🕐 Mon-Tues, Thurs
noon-2am, Wed, Fri-
Sun noon-3am ⓢ $50
Wed (for men only)

JJ's (4, E12)
Not as suity as you might
think – this is disco for

Hong Kong's divine dahlings
with DJs spinning funky
house from 10pm nightly
except Sunday. Dress up (no
shorts, no torn jeans).
✉ Grand Hyatt, 1
Harbour Rd, Wan Chai
☎ 2588 1234 (ext
7323) 🚇 Wan Chai
🕐 Mon-Thurs 5.30pm-
2am, Fri 5.30pm-3am,
Sat 6pm-4am
ⓢ $100-200

KK Disco (3, G7)
This subterranean estab-
lishment is a sea of booths
and tall round tables. The
makeshift dancefloor is
right under the DJ booth,
so you get every encour-
agement to strut your stuff.
✉ Basement, Chevalier
Bldg, 45-51 Chatham
Rd South (enter from
Prat Ave), Tsim Sha
Tsui ☎ 2312 2808
🚇 Tsim Sha Tsui
🕐 6pm-5am ⓢ free

Neptune Disco II
(4, F12) Neptune Disco II
is the spillover bar from the
original (and very seedy)
Neptune around the corner
at 54 Lockhart Rd.
Neptune II is a fun club
with a mostly Filipino
crowd and a rockin' covers
band. If everything's closing and you can't bear to
stop dancing, this is the
place to come.
✉ 98-108 Jaffe Rd,
Wan Chai ☎ 2865
2238 🚇 Wan Chai
🕐 4pm-5am (Fri-Sun
from 2pm) ⓢ $50-150

**Sing-A-Long
Members Club**
(3, G9) This nominally private club will most likely let
you in to partake of its high-
class giggly sleaze where
hostesses are rented by the
minute and drinks are

expensive. There are lavish
banqueted harem-style
lounges. **Club de
Millennium**, on the
10th floor, is the associated
disco.
✉ 9th-11th fl, BCC
Bldg, 25-31 Carnarvon
Rd (enter from Hanoi
Rd), Tsim Sha Tsui
☎ 2368 8013 🚇 Tsim
Sha Tsui ⛴ Star Ferry
🕐 8.30pm-4am
ⓢ around $150

LIVE MUSIC

There is virtually no local original music scene in Hong Kong. The Fringe Club is just about the only place an indie band could play, but it's no CBGBs. Live music usually means Filipino pop bands playing MOR covers in hotel lounges. Worthy local acts include Slow Tech Riddim (groove-electronica), Impersonator (a guitar trio) and Dylan Art (a synth pop duo).

Blue Note (3, H7)
You know they're trying hard when they call their club after the most famous jazz spot in the world. There's mostly imported talent on a rotating residency basis every night except Sunday.
✉ Kowloon Shangri-La Hotel, 64 Mody Rd, Tsim Sha Tsui East ☎ 2721 2111 ⊕ Tsim Sha Tsui ⛴ HKF Hoverferry ⏰ 5pm-1am ⑤ free

Chasers (3, F5)
A friendly, sorta classy pub with a live Filipino covers band every night from 9.30pm. Before the band cranks up, there's a jukebox to party with. Serves a bar menu till midnight and snacks till 4am. There's dancing most nights; weekends see a major sweat-fest.
✉ 2-3 Knutsford Tce,

Tsim Sha Tsui ☎ 2367 9487 ⊕ Tsim Sha Tsui/ Jordan ⏰ 4pm-5am (Sat-Sun from noon) ⑤ free

Dusk till Dawn (4, G12)
Live music from 9.30pm with an emphasis on beats and vibes so irresistible that you'll get your booty shaking. The dance floor can be packed but the atmosphere is usually more friendly than sleazy. Food sticks to easy fillers like meat pies and burgers.
✉ 76-84 Jaffe Rd, Wan Chai ☎ 2528 4689 ⊕ Wan Chai ⏰ Mon-Thurs 4pm-5am, Fri-Sun 2pm-5am ⑤ $100+

Fringe Club (6, E5)
The Fringe, a friendly venue on the border of the Lan Kwai Fong quadrant, has original music in the gallery/bar Friday and

Saturday nights with jazz, rock and world music getting the most airplay. In summer, there's a 'secret' bar on the roof.
✉ 2 Lower Albert Rd, Lan Kwai Fong, Central ☎ 2521 7251 ⊕ Central ⏰ shows Fri & Sat from 10.30pm ⑤ free

Jazz Club (6, D5)
This self-evidently named venue has long been the sole salvation for true music lovers, and many jazz greats have graced its stage. The club also books rock, blues, folk and other kinds of acts, both local and foreign. Book tickets well in advance for the bigger names.
✉ 2nd fl, California Entertainment Bldg, 34 D'Aguilar St, Lan Kwai Fong, Central ☎ 2845 8477 📧 info@lkfgroup .com ⊕ Central ⏰ 5.30pm-1am ⑤ $60-300

The Wanch (4, F11)
The Wanch has live music seven nights a week from 9pm, mostly rock and folk, with the occasional solo guitarist thrown in. Jam night is Monday. If you're not there for the music it's a dubious scene – the Wanch is basically a pick-up joint.
✉ 54 Jaffe Rd, Wan Chai ☎ 2861 1621 ⊕ Wan Chai ⏰ 11am-4am ⑤ free

Major Venues
Though Hong Kong isn't really on the rock circuit, the **HITEC Rotunda** (☎ 2620 2222), 1 Trademark Dr, Wang Chin St, Kowloon Bay, and the **Convention and Exhibition Centre**, in Wan Chai, do host MTV-friendly acts. These venues aren't huge, so tickets can climb to $500. Big international acts also play the **Hong Kong Coliseum** (3, F9; ☎ 2355 7234), 9 Cheong Wan Rd, Hung Hom.

The **Hong Kong Stadium** (see p. 97) is the largest venue for sporting and cultural events. The other mega-venue **Queen Elizabeth Stadium** (3, H15; ☎ 2591 1346) 18 Oi Kwan Rd, Wan Chai, is OK for sports, but lousy for concerts – you'd get better acoustics in an aircraft hangar.

BARS, PUBS & WATERING HOLES

Much of Hong Kong's nightlife takes place in top-end hotels where alluring happy hours, skilled bar staff and some of the best views in town attract visitors and locals. There's also many a stylish bar where the clothes are straight out of the bag, the sounds are smooth, the drinks are electric and the buzz is hardcore gossip. Unsurprisingly, British-style pubs are also plentiful – especially in tourist areas. Often British or Australian owned, they have authentic decor, meat pies, darts and sport on the TV.

STYLE BARS

Antidote (6, C3)
Pure white chill-out bar with a gleaming, trendy mostly Chinese crowd. Lazy during the week, loud and dancey on weekends. Snacks are available.
✉ 15-19 Hollywood Rd (enter from Ezra Lane off Cochrane St), Boho, Central ☎ 2526 6559 Ⓜ Central ⏰ Mon-Thurs 6pm-2am, Fri-Sat 6pm-4am

Area (5, G2)
Seeping blue lights and white chairs make this bar an instant zone. Not large, but smooth and snappy with inventive drinks, slow electronica and a zipless crowd sipping cocktails and nibbling on conversation and snacks.
✉ 21 Sharp St East, Causeway Bay ☎ 2575 6300 Ⓜ Causeway Bay ⏰ 6pm-1am (till 2pm Fri-Sat)

Brecht's (5, G4)
Brecht's is very small and fairly unusual. It's an arty kind of place given more to intimate, cerebral conversation than serious raging. The decor is pseudo-German, and includes oversized portraits of such charmers as Mao and Hitler.
✉ 123 Leighton Rd, Causeway Bay ☎ 2577

9636 (6) Causeway Bay
⏰ Sun-Thurs 4pm-2am, Fri-Sat 4pm-4am

Chemical Suzy
(3, E7) Cyber-groover hide-out with DJs, snacks (scallops, fish fingers) and enough pop culture signifiers to leave no doubt that Suzy's in the know.
✉ AWT Centre, 2 Austin Ave, Tsim Sha Tsui ☎ 2736 0087 Ⓜ Tsim Sha Tsui ⏰ Mon-Sat 6pm-4am, Sun 9pm-4am

Club Feather Boa
(6, C2) Feather Boa is a plush lounge hidden behind gold drapes. The scenario is 'trashy princess meets dilapidated gentleman for a cocktail but ends up drinking bottled beer from a chunky stemmed glass'.
✉ 38 Staunton St, Soho, Central ☎ 2857 2586 Ⓜ Central/Sheung Wan ⏰ 6.30pm-late

D.Bar (5, G4)
Snug in a strip of motorcycle workshops, this is a colourful low-key nook with a sociable padded bench down one side, cartoons on the monitors and no fear of disco.
✉ 13 Caroline Hill Rd, Causeway Bay ☎ 2882 2020 Ⓜ Causeway Bay ⏰ 5pm-1am

Tsingtao and San Miguel compete with Carlsberg and Löwenbrau for the affections of HK's beer fans.

La Dolce Vita (6, D5)
A buzzing place for post-work brews with room to bar-prop or stand on the terrace and watch the mob crawl by. Gets a bit messy on weekends.
✉ Cosmos Bldg, 9-11 Lan Kwai Fong, Lan Kwai Fong, Central ☎ 2186 1888 Ⓜ Central ⏰ 9am-2am (till 4pm Fri-Sat)

Le Jardin (6, D4)

Don't imagine a breezy garden – the 'jardin' is an enclosed verandah – but this is still an attractive bar with loads of atmosphere. The mostly expat crowd enjoys itself without getting too boisterous.

✉ 1st fl, Winner Bldg, 10 Wing Wah Lane, Lan Kwai Fong, Central ☎ 2526 2717 ⊕ Central ⏲ noon-2am

Oscar's (6, D5)

High-fashion watering hole and restaurant where you can play 'spot the model'. There's a second location in the World Trade Centre, Podium 3, 280 Gloucester Rd, Causeway Bay.

✉ 2 Lan Kwai Fong, Lan Kwai Fong, Central ☎ 2804 6561 ⊕ Central ⏲ 11am-11pm (Sun till 10pm)

Phi-B (6, C4)

Trendy orange and turquoise bar where you can kick off the night or bring the pace down. When the DJ pumps it up, the crowd spills onto the front steps for stargazing and air-gulping. Free snacks during happy hour (5-9pm).

✉ Harilela House, 79 Wyndham St (enter off Pottinger St), Boho, Central ☎ 2869 4469

High Phi-b

⊕ Central ⏲ Mon-Thurs 5pm-2am, Fri-Sat 5pm-5am

Staunton's Wine Bar & Café (6, C2)

Staunton's is swish, cool and on the ball with ice-clinking drinks, an escalator-watching scene and live jazz most evenings. For eats, there's expensive focaccia downstairs and a modern international restaurant upstairs.

✉ 10-12 Staunton St (cnr Shelley St), Soho, Central ☎ 2973 6611 ⊕ Central ⏲ 9am-midnight

Face up to it!

Visage Free (6, C3)

Cheerful Boho bar which defies its dungeon setting. It's far less trendy than most bars around here, maintaining a low-key feel with occasional poetry readings and a loyal

regular crowd.

✉ Amber Lodge, 23 Hollywood Rd (enter from Cochrane St), Boho, Central ☎ 2546 9780 ⊕ Central ⏲ 5pm-1am (later Fri & Sat)

HOTEL BARS

The Bar (3, J5)

For mellow 1940s and 50s jazz, take your smoking jacket along and sip cognac at The Bar. Your fellow tipplers will be serious business types, coutured couples and new money trying to look old. The music starts around 9.30pm.

✉ The Peninsula (cnr Salisbury & Nathan Rds), Tsim Sha Tsui ☎ 2315 3135 ⊕ Tsim Sha Tsui ⚓ Star Ferry ⏲ noon-1am

Captain's Bar (4, E6)

This is a clubby, suited place which serves ice-cold draught beer in chilled silver mugs. Butlers bring lunch and afternoon tea buffets and set them up in the bar. This is a good place to talk business, at least until the covers band strikes up at 9pm.

✉ Mandarin Oriental Hotel, 5 Connaught Rd, Central ☎ 2522 0111 ⊕ Central ⏲ 11am-2am

Club Shanghai (3, K6)

Club Shanghai is quite posh with a 1930s Shanghai theme, right down to the (empty) opium pipes on each table. An American house band pumps out dance tunes six nights a week.

✉ 1st fl, Regent Hotel, 18 Salisbury Rd, Tsim Sha Tsui ☎ 2721 1211 ⊕ Tsim Sha Tsui

⚓ **Star Ferry** ◷ Mon-Thurs 8pm-1am, Fri-Sat 8pm-2am

Cyrano's (4, G8)

If you like to get high while you drink, come visit Cyrano's for expert bartenders, Continental meals and live jazz (from 9pm). Change lifts at the 36th floor for a good atrium view on the way up.
✉ **56th fl, Island Shangri-La Hotel, Supreme Court Rd, Admiralty** ☎ 2820 8591 ⊖ **Admiralty** ◷ Mon-Sat 7-9am, noon-3pm, 5pm-1.30am, Sun 7-10am, 11.30am-1.30am ♿ yes

Hari's (3, H5)

Tacky or classy? You decide, after you've had a couple of speciality martinis (there are over a dozen to challenge you, including wasabi and garlic). Happy hours are Monday-Saturday 5-9pm and all night Sunday. There's live music nightly: it's covers Monday-Saturday and 'folk classics' Sunday.
✉ **Mezzanine, Holiday Inn Golden Mile, 50 Nathan Rd, Tsim Sha Tsui** ☎ 2369 3111 (ext 1345) ⊖ **Tsim Sha Tsui** ◷ 6pm-2am

Sky Lounge (3, J5)

Before you can criticise the departure lounge feel of this big, long bar you've already started marvelling at the view. Don't take flight: sit down in a scoop chair, sip a drink and scoff international snacks.
✉ **18th fl, Sheraton Hotel & Towers, 20 Nathan Rd, Tsim Sha Tsui** ☎ 2369 1111 ⊖ **Tsim Sha Tsui** ⚓ **Star Ferry** ◷ 2pm-1am, (till 2am Fri-Sat) ♿ yes

PUBS & WATERING HOLES

Biergarten (3, H6)

This clean place has a hits-and-memories jukebox and Bitburger on tap. It's popular with visiting Germans and others who hanker after Black Forest ham, smoked pork loin and schnitzels. This is a nonthreatening place to have a solo beer – on fine days, the front is opened to the street.
✉ **5 Hanoi Rd, Tsim Sha Tsui** ☎ 2721 2302 ⊖ **Tsim Sha Tsui** ◷ noon-2am

Bit Point (6, D5)

Owned by the same people as Biergarten, Bit Point and nearby **Schnurrbart** draw fans of German beer who like a rowdy drinking atmosphere. Most beers here are draught pilsners (which you can get in a glass boot if you've got a huge thirst to kick).
✉ **31 D'Aguilar St, Lan Kwai Fong, Central** ☎ 2523 7436 ⊖ **Central** ◷ Mon-Thurs 11am-1am, Fri-Sat 11am-3am, Sun 6pm-midnight

Club 1911 (6, C2)

A refined bar with art nouveau details steeped in colonial nostalgia. If you get the munchies, you can order in food from some of the surrounding eateries. Happy hour is 5-9pm.
✉ **27 Staunton St, Soho, Central** ☎ 2810 6681 ⊖ **Central** ◷ Mon-Sat 5pm-midnight

Club 64 (6, D4)

This funky hang-out is apparently named after the Tiananmen Square massacre (64 stands for the date of the massacre on the 4th of the 6th month, or 4 June). As a sign of the times, the graffiti (in English and Chinese) that once covered the walls has been whitewashed over. This is still one of the best bars in town for those who want simple, unfussy fun.
✉ **Winner Bldg, 12 Wing Wah Lane, Lan Kwai Fong, Central** ☎ 2523 2801 ⊖ **Central** ◷ 3pm-1am (till 3pm Fri-Sat)

Drinking dens abound in Hong Kong town.

Delaney's (4, G12)

Delaney's is an incongruously located – yet immensely popular – Irish pub. It's worth the effort to find, as you can order a draught Guinness poured with the care and expertise it deserves. For a change of pace, try Delaney's Ale, a house brew made by the South China Brewing Co. The food is good too – the kitchen goes through 400kg of potatoes a week!
✉ **2nd fl, One Capital Place, 18 Luard Rd, Wan Chai (also 3-7 Prat Ave, Tsim Sha Tsui)** ☎ 2804 2880 ⊖ **Wan Chai** ◷ noon-late

Godown (4, F7)

An all-day bar and restaurant which starts with breakfast and ploughs on bravely until late-night snacks. There are speciality beers on tap and a comfortably dim bar.

✉ **Basement, Citibank Plaza, 3 Garden Rd, Central** ☎ **2523 8893** ⓜ **Central** ⏱ **Mon-Sat 7am-midnight**

Jungle Pub (4, G12)

Lively drinking cellar which is popular with local Chinese folk who pay more attention to the labels on their beer bottles than those on their clothes. Weekends get rowdy in a nice kind of way.

✉ **Basement, Heng Shun Mansion, 76-82 Jaffe Rd, Wan Chai** ☎ **2529 1828** ⓜ **Wan Chai** ⏱ **noon-2am**

Hop on in.

Kangaroo Pub

(3, G4) The infamous Kangaroo is the bane of Australian expats struggling to prove that not all their countrymen are lager louts. This place gets pretty lively, and there are some

Body armour not required

decent Aussie beers like Cooper's and VB. This is where you come to watch Aussie Rules and rugby on satellite TV.

✉ **1st & 2nd fl, Daily House, 35 Haiphong Rd, Tsim Sha Tsui** ☎ **2376 0083** ⓜ **Tsim Sha Tsui** ⏱ **Mon-Sat 7-9am, noon-3pm, 5pm-1.30am, Sun 7-10am, 11.30am-1.30am**

LA Cafe (4, F8)

The LA Cafe has a large, loyal following of late-night revellers. A sports-bar mentality is in evidence: there are booths, a long bar, lots of TVs and a 3-9pm happy hour. On weekends, Club Lollipop takes over the dance floor with 70s & 80s hits (9pm-2am). The mostly Mexican luncheons are not to be overlooked either.

✉ **Shop 2-3, Lippo Centre, 89 Queensway, Admiralty** ☎ **2526 6863** ⓜ **Admiralty** ⏱ **Mon-Tues 11am-11.30pm, Fri-Sat 11am-12.30am, Sun 10am-11.30pm** ♿ **yes**

Lord Stanley's

(2, E4) Foreigners' bar with all-day breakfast and bar food. The TVs are usually glued to some kind of sport. It's cosy and quiet during the week but the drunken lords have been

known to spill out into the street on weekends.

✉ **92a Stanley Main St, Stanley** ☎ **2813 9130** ⓜ **Stanley** ⏱ **Mon-Thurs 10am-1am, Fri-Sun 10am-2am** ♿ **yes**

Ned Kelly's Last Stand (3, H4)

Ashley Rd has its own little time warp in this tribute to the 19th-century Australian bushranger and folk hero. A great tradition continues with the Kelly Gang playing Dixieland jazz nightly till 2am. Food is available and there's never a cover charge.

✉ **11a Ashley Rd, Tsim Sha Tsui** ☎ **2376 0562** ⓜ **Tsim Sha Tsui** ⏱ **11.30am-2am** ♿ **yes**

Oddfellas (1, D8)

Expat sports bar with all-day snacks and meals including Aussie steaks and American burgers. Slip next door to the swish attached restaurant if you'd rather romantic candlelight than TV glare illuminating your dinner.

✉ **55-57 Yi Chun St, Sai Kung** ☎ **2791 4123** ⓔ **oddfellaspub@ yahoo.com** ⓜ **Choi Hung (then bus 92 or minibus 1, 1a, 4)** ⏱ **noon-2am** ♿ **yes**

SPECTATOR SPORT

Basketball

The Asian Basketball Association plays some matches in Hong Kong between May and July.

Cricket

The HK International Cricket Series is held in late September to early October. This 2-day event at the Hong Kong Stadium sees teams from Australia, England, India, New Zealand, Pakistan and the West Indies battle it out in a speedy version of the game.

Horse Racing

Without a doubt, horse races are Hong Kong's biggest spectator sport. There are about 65 meetings a year at two racecourses, Hong Kong Island's **Happy Valley** (see p. 15) and **Sha Tin** (1, D7) in the New Territories. The racing season is from late September to June. Normally, races at Sha Tin are held on Saturday from 1 to 6pm. The HKTA has 'Come Horse Racing Tours' to Happy Valley and Sha Tin. See page 54 for details.

Rugby

The Seven-A-Side Rugby Tournament, popularly known as the Rugby Sevens, sees teams from all over the world come together in Hong Kong every March (or early April) for three days of lightning-fast (15mins) matches. Even non-rugby fans scramble to get tickets, for in addition to the sport, there's a lot of action in the stands.

Matches are held at the **Hong Kong Stadium** (5, J5; ☎ 2895 7895), 55 Eastern Hospital Road, So Kan Po, but getting tickets isn't easy: ask the HKTA or the HK Rugby Football Union (☎ 2504 8311), Sports House, 1 Stadium Path, So Kon Po.

Hong Kong Tourist Association

Catch!

Soccer

Hong Kong has a fairly lively amateur soccer league. Games are played on pitches inside the Happy Valley Horse Racing Track and at Mong Kok Stadium. The sports section of the English-language papers carries information on when and where matches are held. Or contact the Hong Kong Football Association (☎ 2712 9122), 55 Fat Kwong St, Ho Man Tin, Kowloon.

Tennis

Several international tennis tournaments are held annually in Hong Kong, the largest in April. The tournaments are held in Victoria Park (5, E5) in Causeway Bay. Check the local newspapers for details.

places to stay

With the exception of screechingly lovely high-end joints, Hong Kong's hotels tend to impress only with their numbing sameness or, at the bottom end, with their resemblance to musty cupboards. But with over 35,000 rooms and occupancy usually under 90%, you should find a suitable temporary residence here.

Hong Kong's two high seasons are March-April and October-November. Outside of these periods, rates tend to drop and happy bonuses can come your way: airport transport, room upgrades, late checkout, free breakfast and complimentary cocktails. If the hotel seems a bit quiet when you arrive, it can be worth asking for a upgrade.

Room Rates

These categories indicate the cost per night of a standard double room:

Deluxe $2800 and over
Top End $1200-2799
Mid-Range $800-1199
Budget $799 and under

Add 3% tax and, usually, a 10% service charge to quoted rates.

Hong Kong Tourist Association

Hong Kong's deluxe hotels are special places, with individual qualities that propel them above the rest. Expect discreet, personalised service, large baths, superlative climate control, extensive cable TV with Internet access, dataports and fax machines. Top end hotels are in spiffing locations: they also have smart, comfortable rooms with excellent air-con, inhouse movies and a good variety of room service. Amenities include business facilities, bars and restaurants and fluent English-speaking staff.

Mid-range hotels tend to be generic business/tourist establishments with little to distinguish one from another. Rooms are spacious enough (if you don't plan on playing Twister of an evening), and usually have a bath, limited cable TV and room service. The majority of Hong Kong's budget digs are in Kowloon, a lot of it on or near Nathan Rd. Though most budget rooms are very small, the places listed here are clean and cheerily shabby rather than grim and grimy. The hotels we've included all have private bathrooms, telephones, TVs and air-conditioning.

Special Deals

The best rates at the better hotels tend to come through travel agents and booking services. Also check flight and accommodation packages in advance, or visit the Hotels Association counter at the airport on arrival. The HKTA doesn't book rooms, but hotels advertise special deals via its Web site (www.hkta.org/hotels). For mid-range and top end discounted rates try a hotel room consolidator such as Traveller Services (☎ 2375 2222; fax 2375 2233; www. traveller.com.hk) .

Watery blue view from the Regent

DELUXE

Island Shangri-La

(4, G8) A sterile exterior here conceals swisho sophistication. Personal service is key: staff seem genuinely interested in making your stay pleasant. Nice touches include a library where you can take afternoon tea, an outdoor spa and a 24hr business centre. Half-hourly shuttles service the Convention Centre and the Star Ferry.
✉ **Pacific Place, Supreme Court Rd, Admiralty** ☎ **2877 3838; fax 2521 8742** e **isl@shangri-la.com; www.shangri-la.com** ⊕ **Admiralty**

Mandarin Oriental

(4, E6) This, the Peninsula's HK Island counterpart, is not architecturally as impressive but has a healthy dose of old-world charm. Styling is subdued, and sometimes a bit outdated, but the service, food, atmosphere and views are excellent. Rooms have Internet-capable TVs with cordless keyboards for bedside browsing.
✉ **5 Connaught Rd, Central** ☎ **2522 0111; fax 2810 6190** e **reserve-mohkg@ mohg.com; www .mandarinoriental.com** ⊕ **Central** ⚓ **Star Ferry**

JW Marriot (4, G9)

Though business-traveller focussed, it's also popular with shopoholics who feed their addiction next door at Pacific Place. Well-appointed rooms are drenched in that special hush you only get in top hotels. The cheaper city side rooms have hill views (rather than air-con infrastructure vistas).
✉ **Pacific Place, 88 Queensway, Admiralty** ☎ **2841 3000; fax 2845 0737** e **room@marriott .com.hk; www.marriott .com** ⊕ **Admiralty**

The throne-like Peninsula

The Peninsula (3, J5)

Pure colonial elegance awaits in this throne-like structure. Classic European-style rooms boast faxes, VCRs, CD players and marble bathrooms. Newer wing rooms can offer spectacular harbour views; in the original building, you'll have to make do with interior sumptuousness. See p. 26.
✉ **Cnr Salisbury & Nathan Rds, Tsim Sha Tsui** ☎ **2920 2888; fax 2722 4170** e **pen@peninsula.com; www.peninsula.com** ⊕ **Tsim Sha Tsui** ⚓ **Star Ferry**

Regent Hotel (3, K6)

The Regent tilts at modernity while bowing to colonial traditions such as a fleet of Rolls Royces, uniformed doormen and incessant brass polishing. The impeccable emphasis on service ensures a lot of return leisure and business custom. The restaurants are superb and the foyer bar has the best view in town. Even if you don't stay, drop by for a bevvy.
✉ **18 Salisbury Rd, Tsim Sha Tsui** ☎ **2721 1211; fax 2739 4546** e **reservations.rhk@ fourseasons.com; www.regenthotels.com** ⊕ **Tsim Sha Tsui** ⚓ **Star Ferry**

Renaissance Harbour View (4, E12)

This spectacular hotel adjoins the Convention & Exhibition Centre, ensuring steady suit-and-tie custom. Deal-cutters are catered to with a well-equipped business centre and discreet restaurants. Leisure travellers will appreciate informed concierges and, perhaps, the flashy nightclub. It has the largest of all outdoor pools overlooking the harbour and a kiddies pool as well.
✉ **1 Harbour Rd, Wan Chai** ☎ **2802 8888; fax 2802 8833** e **rhvhksal @hkstar.com; www .renaissancehotels.com** ⊕ **Wan Chai** ⚓ **Star Ferry**

Ritz-Carlton (4, E7)

A truly beautiful hotel with plush rooms that manage to be cosy and incredibly distinguished all at once. Views from harbour-side rooms are – no surprise – breathtaking but the best views might be from the pool: lay back and soak up the skyline.
✉ **3 Connaught Rd, Central** ☎ **2877 6666; fax 2877 6778** e **ritzrchk@hk.super.net; www.ritzcarlton.com** ⊕ **Central** ⚓ **Star Ferry**

TOP END

Century Harbour Hotel

(2, C2) New hotel with a lot going for it. The location is not so convenient but the views from the harbourside rooms, the 28th floor Moon Bar and rooftop pool are great. A pleasing attention to detail shows in the good-sized baths and stylish trimmings throughout.

✉ 508 Queen's Rd West, Western ☎ 2974 1234; fax 2974 0333 e harbour_hotel@ century.com.hk; www .century-harbour-hotel .com 🚌 5, 10, 47a, 101, 104 🚇 Hill Rd stop, walk south to Queen's Rd West

Excelsior Hotel (5, E3)

While the Excelsior can't help but absorb some of the buzz of its retail-mad location, it also maintains a haven-like serenity. It's modern, efficient, arty and trendy with good restaurants, a tennis court, business centre and fab views from harbour view rooms.

✉ 281 Gloucester Rd, Causeway Bay ☎ 2894 8888; fax 2895 6459 e booking@exhkg.com.hk; www.mandarinoriental. com 🚇 Causeway Bay

Holiday Inn Golden Mile (3, H5)

This businesslike hotel isn't a bad place to base yourself. Rooms are Holiday Inn reliable and there's the brilliant Avenue Restaurant and schmoozy Hari's bar on-site.

✉ 50 Nathan Rd (cnr Mody Rd), Tsim Sha Tsui ☎ 2369 3111; fax 2369 8016 e reserv@goldenmile .com; www.goldenmile .com 🚇 Tsim Sha Tsui

You are entering the Hyatt sci-fi movie-set zone.

Hyatt Regency (3, H4)

The towering Hyatt is slightly lower priced than the rest of the deluxe deck and the staff are not at all snooty. Its Chinese Restaurant is justly revered and the Hyatt also wins for having one of the cheesiest bars in Hong Kong: the Chin Chin bar with a shaken-not-stirred 1960s vibe.

✉ 67 Nathan Rd (cnr Peking Rd), Tsim Sha Tsui ☎ 2311 1234; fax 2739 8701 e general @hyattregency.com.hk; www.hyatt.com 🚇 Tsim Sha Tsui

The Kowloon will keep you dry and high.

Kowloon Hotel (3, J4)

Part of the Peninsula stable, the Kowloon has a second-string feel, with its comically ostentatious lobby and great views of … the back

of the Peninsula Hotel. Nevertheless, the hotel is popular for its unflappable service, decent rooms and the fab dim sum served in the basement restaurant.

✉ 19-21 Nathan Rd (cnr Middle Rd), Tsim Sha Tsui ☎ 2929 2888; fax 2739 9811 e khh@peninsula.com 🚇 Tsim Sha Tsui 🚢 Star Ferry

Marco Polo Hotel

(3, G3) The lynchpin in the Marco Polo Hotel group's Canton Rd trio, the Marco Polo is a flash hotel with good business facilities. The **Hong Kong Hotel**, a little closer to the Star Ferry, is a bit more salubrious and slightly higher priced; it's has an outdoor pool. **The Prince**, at the northern end of Harbour City, is the slick younger brother with smart newly renovated rooms. If you stayed in one of these hotels, you could do all your shopping, eating and entertaining in Harbour City and never go outdoors.

✉ 3 Canton Rd, Harbour City, Tsim Sha Tsui ☎ 2113 0888; fax 2113 0022 e mphkgbc@wlink.net; www.marcopolohotels .com 🚇 Tsim Sha Tsui 🚢 Star Ferry

New World Hotel

(3, J6) This Kowloon stalwart is popular with European group tours. Rooms with harbour views speak for themselves; infacing rooms are a little disappointing. There's an outdoor pool set in a huge but somewhat unkempt garden with a spectacular view.

✉ 22 Salisbury Rd, Tsim Sha Tsui ☎ 2369 4111; fax 2369 9387 @ nwrhk1@netvigator .com ⊙ Tsim Sha Tsui 🛳 HKF Hoverferry

Regal Airport Hotel

(1, E2) An easy undercover shuffle from the airport terminal, this is a stylish hotel with sleek, comfy rooms, many with futuristic runway views. There's a splashy indoor/outdoor pool complex, half a dozen restaurants and fun games rooms (one for adults, one for kids). Soundproofing ensures the only noise is of your own making, protecting you from jet noise and also from occasional rave parties in the ballroom downstairs.

✉ 9 Cheong Tat Rd, Airport, Chek Lap Kok ☎ 2286 8888; fax 2286 8686 @ regalrah@ netvigator.com; www.regal-hotels.com ⊙ Tung Chung MTR (then bus E31, S51, S61) 🚆 Airport Express 🚌 A21, E31, S51, S61, S64

Royal Garden Hotel

(3, G7) Certainly the best-equipped hotel in Tsim Sha Tsui East and one of Hong Kong's most attractive options overall. From the chic blonde wood and chrome lobby to the rooftop sports complex (25m pool, putting green and tennis court with million dollar views), the Royal Garden kicks goals. The tasteful, freshly-renovated rooms lead off a spacey central atrium.

✉ 69 Mody Rd, Tsim Sha Tsui East ☎ 2721 5215; fax 2369 9976 @ htlinfo@rghk.com.hk; www.theroyalgarden hotel.com.hk ⊙ Tsim Sha Tsui 🛳 HKF Hoverferry

MID-RANGE

Concourse Hotel

(2, B2) Popular with tourists from mainland China, this hotel scrambles at the edge of stylishness but ends up excelling at adequacy. The neighbourhood is loud but you're very close to the MTR if you need to escape.

✉ 20 Lai Chi Kok Rd (near Prince Edward Rd W), Mong Kok ☎ 2397 6683; fax 2381 3768 @ info@hotelconcourse .com.hk; www.hotelcon course.com.hk ⊙ Prince Edward 🚌 2, 2a

Empire Hotel

(4, G11) With its sunny staff, pleasant rooms and small pool on the 21st floor terrace, the Empire is a good option close to the Convention Centre. The extra steps it takes are modest but endearing (eg, free apples at reception). Ask about the group's new hotel in Tsim Sha Tsui.

✉ 33 Hennessy Rd (cnr Fenwick St), Wan Chai ☎ 2866 9111; fax 2861 3121 @ ehhresa@asia standard.com; www. asiastandard.com ⊙ Wan Chai 🚆 Fenwick St

Imperial Hotel (3, H5)

Unrenovated rooms with faded pink bathrooms might be off-putting but they're prim, proper and squeaky clean. It's so well located that the noise of Nathan Rd leaks into the street-facing rooms – take a back room if you sleep light.

✉ 30-34 Nathan Rd, Tsim Sha Tsui ☎ 2366 2201; fax 2311 2360 @ imperial@imperial hotel.com.hk; www .imperialhotel.com.hk ⊙ Tsim Sha Tsui

Kimberley Hotel

(3, F6) It isn't even slightly glam but it's one of the better mid-range hotels in Tsim Sha Tsui with assured staff and more than adequate rooms and facilities (including golf nets). The suites all have kitchenettes.

✉ 28 Kimberley Rd, Tsim Sha Tsui ☎ 2723 3888; fax 2723 1318 @ kh-rsvn@kimberley .com.hk; www.kimberley .com.hk ⊙ Tsim Sha Tsui

Luk Kwok Hotel

(4, F12) This is a relatively small, not many frills, no harbour views kinda place (though they talk up their city and mountain aspects). Staff are keen and helpful and you're close to the Convention Centre, Star Ferry and Wan Chai's bustle.

✉ 72 Gloucester Rd, Wan Chai ☎ 2866 2166; fax 2866 2622 @ lukkwok@lukkwok hotel.com ⊙ Wan Chai

New Astor Hotel

(3, H5) If you want to walk out of your hotel and get a faceful of Hong Kong, this could be the place. It's close to Nathan Rd and right in the epicentre of the shopping mayhem of Carnarvon and Granville Rds. The rooms are reasonably priced and adequately appointed.
✉ **11 Carnarvon Rd, Tsim Sha Tsui** ☎ **2366 7261; fax 2722 7122** e **hotel@newastor .com.hk; www.newastor .com.hk** Ⓜ **Tsim Sha Tsui**

Park Hotel (3, G6)

The Park is busy and congenial with slightly dated but by no means grotty rooms of good size. Family suites are available. The History and Science museums are just over the road; the hustle of Granville Rd is a block away.
✉ **61-65 Chatham Rd South, Tsim Sha Tsui East** ☎ **2366 1371; fax 2739 7259** e **park2@chevalier.net** Ⓜ **Tsim Sha Tsui**

Pearl Seaview Hotel

(3, A4) Ambitiously named hotel which does big trade in Chinese group tours. The rooms are fine, but not so delightful that they'll keep you inside: Temple St Market and Nathan Rd retail are within easy reach, while the

Tin Hau Temple is practically at the front door.
✉ **262-276 Shanghai St (cnr Public Square St), Yau Ma Tei** ☎ **2782 0882; fax 2388 1803** Ⓜ **Yau Ma Tei**

Royal Pacific Hotel & Towers (3, G2)

Choose between cheaper rooms in the hotel section or flashier rooms in the harbour-facing tower. The location is good: there's a walkway to Kowloon Park, leading onto Nathan Rd and the MTR station. At rear, the hotel is connected to the China/Macau Ferry Terminal. It's also a mere skedaddle to the shopping overkill of Harbour City.
✉ **33 Canton Rd, Tsim Sha Tsui** ☎ **2736 1188; fax 2736 1212** e **room@ymcahk .org.hk** Ⓜ **Tsim Sha Tsui** ⚓ **Macau Ferry**

Royal Plaza Hotel

(2, B2) The plushness is a bit overdone but it has to be admitted that the Plaza is comfortable. We love the heated no-steam bathroom mirrors and the large, loungey outdoor pool. The Mong Kok KCR station is accessible through the adjoining shopping centre, making this a handy spot if you've business in the New Territories or China.
✉ **193 Prince Edward**

Rd West, Mong Kok ☎ **2928 8822; fax 2606 0088** e **resvn@ royalplaza.com.hk; www.royalplaza.com.hk** Ⓜ **Prince Edward** 🚉 **Mong Kok KCR**

Stanford Hillview Hotel (3, E6)

A decent place to swag near the food, fun and all night dancing of Knutsford Terrace but set back from the Nathan Rd jabber. The rooms are forgettable but fine.
✉ **13-17 Observatory Rd (cnr Knutsford Tce), Tsim Sha Tsui** ☎ **2722 7822; fax 2723 3718** e **hillview@stanford hotel.com; www.stan fordhillview.com** Ⓜ **Tsim Sha Tsui**

Wharney Hotel

(4, G11) The Wharney is noteworthy for its outdoor whirlpool and swimming pool. The so-called Departure Lounge offers nice respite for weary departing guests awaiting late-night flights. Bonus feature: cricket fans can pretend they're staying with a smokin' Aussie leg spinner.
✉ **61-73 Lockhart Rd, Wan Chai** ☎ **2861 1000; fax 2529 5133** e **wharney@wlink.net** Ⓜ **Wan Chai** 🚉 **Fenwick St or Luard Rd St**

Serviced Apartments

A mostly post-colonial innovation, there are some excellent serviced apartments springing up. One of the newest is **22 Peel** (6, B3; ☎ 2522 3082; fax 2522 2762). These chic pads are in the rapidly changing Soho district, a mere tumble down the hill to Central. Ranging from fairly spacious studio flats to 2-bedroom apartments, they're all tastefully furnished and exceedingly comfortable. Features include broadband Internet connection, DVD library, wine cellar and membership of the nearby New York Fitness Club (p. 45). Prices kick off at around $20,000/month.

BUDGET

BP International House
(3, E3) The International House is at the top end of Kowloon Park, 5mins from the outdoor swimming complex and a short walk to Nathan Rd and Jordan MTR. The rooms are dowdy but comfortable; some of the more expensive rooms have good harbour views. They have bunk rooms, making this a good option if you're travelling with kids or in a group.
✉ **8 Austin Rd, Tsim Sha Tsui ☎ 2376 1111; fax 2376 1333**
e bpi.reservations @megahotels.com.hk; www.megahotels.com.hk
Ⓜ Jordan

Booth Lodge (3, A4)
Run by the Salvation Army, Booth Lodge is appropriately spartan, but clean and comfortable. There is efficient air-con (you can't open the windows), a pleasant cafe and disabled access. Room rates include breakfast. Note that reception is on the 7th floor.
✉ **11 Wing Sing Lane, Yau Ma Tei ☎ 2771 9266; fax 2385 1140**
Ⓜ **Yau Ma Tei**
🚌 1, 1a, 2, 6, 6a

Caritas Bianchi Lodge
(3, A5) Nonprofit lodge with straightforward, fairly spacious rooms. Though it's just off Nathan Rd (and a goalie's throw from Yau Ma Tei MTR) the rear rooms are very quiet and some have views onto Kings Park.
✉ **4 Cliff Rd, Yau Ma Tei ☎ 2388 1111; fax 2770 6669** **e** cblresv @bianchi-lodge.com
Ⓜ **Yau Ma Tei**
🚌 1, 1a, 2, 6, 6a

Caritas Lodge (2, B2)
Caritas Lodge is not as central as its sister hotel (it's a brisk 10mins walk to the MTR) but it's cheaper and the linoleum-floored rooms are clean and liveable, if a bit noisy. There's a church, school, community centre and cafe on site, giving the place a bustling workaday feel.
✉ **134 Boundary St (near Waterloo Rd), Mong Kok ☎ 2339 3777; fax 2338 2864**
e reservationtas-lodge .com Ⓜ Prince Edward
🚌 1, 1a

Chungking House
(3, H5) You're in the hell that is Chungking Mansions but this 'deluxe hostel' is bearable if you're on a budget. The rooms are clean enough and bigger than many in this complex. If you get one looking over Nathan Rd you can just about convince yourself it's exotic.
✉ **A Block, Chungking Mansions, 40 Nathan Rd, Tsim Sha Tsui ☎ 2366 5362; fax 2721 3570**
Ⓜ **Tsim Sha Tsui**

Garden View International House (YWCA) (4, H5)
Hovering on the border of Central and the Mid-Levels, the Garden View overlooks the Zoo & Botanical Gardens. It's the only place in the area that falls outside the luxury category. Accommodation is plain but comfortable (there's good air-conditioning) and there's an outdoor swimming pool.
✉ **1 MacDonnell Rd, Central ☎ 2877 3737; fax 2845 6263** **e** gar_view@ywca.org.hk; www.ywca.org.hk
🚌 12a, minibus 1a

Goodrich Hotel (3, C4)
The inviting, air-conditioned lobby is let down by the stuffy, slightly shabby rooms. Nevertheless, you can't knock Goodrich for value or location: it's right near the Temple St market and Jordan MTR. The quoted rates seem pretty liquid – try negotiating.
✉ **92-94 Woosung St, Tsim Sha Tsui ☎ 2332 2020; fax 2332 3138** **e** goodrichhotel@goodrich hotel.com.hk Ⓜ Jordan

Escape the traffic din inside the Nathan.

John Hay

Harbour View International House (Chinese YMCA)

(4, F12) Right next door to the Hong Kong Arts Centre and a mere stroll to the Convention Centre and Wan Chai ferry terminal, this is a great value choice for its location. Most of the Harbour View's simply furnished but perfectly adequate rooms look out over Victoria Harbour.

✉ 4 Harbour Rd, Wan Chai ☎ 2802 0111; fax 2802 9063 ℮ hvihymca @netvigator.com; www. harbour.ymca.org.hk
Ⓜ Wan Chai

Kowloon & New Garden Hotels

(3, H5) These hotels in the Mirador Arcade share the same phone and owner. Clean but stuffy singles and doubles with tiny private toilet/shower closet are $180 (cheaper without a window). Rooms have phones and a small TV. The lifts here are slow but you can glory in the fact that they're better than the diabolical Chungking lifts.

✉ Mirador Arcade, 58 Nathan Rd, Tsim Sha Tsui ☎ 2311 2523; fax 2368 5241 Ⓜ Tsim Sha Tsui

Nathan Hotel

(3, B4) The Nathan is surprisingly quiet and pleasant; even the cheapest rooms are spacious, clean and serene. It has triples available and is in a good location, right near the Jordan MTR station and the Temple St night market.

✉ 378 Nathan Rd, Yau Ma Tei ☎ 2388 5141; fax 2770 4262 ℮ nathanhk@hkstar.com
Ⓜ Yau Ma Tei/Jordan

Wish on the Shamrock and you'll be in luck.

Newton Hotel Kowloon

(2, B2) Not a bad option if you don't mind being in a very local and head-under-pillow noisy neighbourhood. The MTR is a 5min-walk away and you're close to the Mong Kong fresh food market, clothes stalls and noodle houses. The hotel itself is fair enough for the price – no surprises.

✉ 66 Boundary St (cnr Sai Yee St), Mong Kok ☎ 2787 2338; fax 2789 0688 ℮ newton kln@hmhm-group.com
Ⓜ Prince Edward
🚌 1, 1a

Salisbury YMCA Hotel

(3, J4) If you manage to book a room here, you'll be rewarded with professional service and excellent exercise facilities. The rooms are comfortable, if somewhat worn, but you won't mind if you keep your eyes on the harbour view. (Gloat factor: the same view is much more expensive at next door's Peninsula.) Family rooms and four-bed dorms are available.

✉ 41 Salisbury Rd, Tsim Sha Tsui ☎ 2268 7888; fax 2739 9315 ℮ room@ymcahk.org.hk; www.ymcahk.org.hk
Ⓜ Tsim Sha Tsui
⛴ Star Ferry

Shamrock Hotel

(3, D4) The Shamrock is fantastic value. The beds can be a bit spongy but the rooms are well-sized, clean and airy, and there are excellent kitsch lounges outside the lifts. The MTR is right outside the door and there's a cheap, decent restaurant on site.

✉ 223 Nathan Rd, Tsim Sha Tsui ☎ 2735 2271; fax 2736 7354 ℮ shamrock@iohk.com; www.yp.com.hk/sham rock Ⓜ Jordan

'It's fun to stay at the...' YMCAs in Hong Kong.

facts for the visitor

John Hay

ARRIVAL & DEPARTURE

Almost all international travellers arrive and depart via Chek Lap Kok airport. Travellers to and from mainland China can use ferry or rail links to Guangzhou and beyond. It's also possible to fly or drive into Macau and catch a ferry from there.

Air

Hong Kong's sleek Chek Lap Kok airport (1, E2) is built on a huge slab of reclaimed land to the north of hilly Lantau Island. It opened in 1998, replacing the old Kai Tak airport in suburban Kowloon.

The airport is connected to the mainland by the 2.2km-long Tsing Ma Bridge, one of the world's longest suspension bridges, linking the islands of Tsing Yi and Ma Wan. Highways and a flashy fast train link the airport with Kowloon and Hong Kong.

Information

General Inquiries
☎ 2181 0000

Flight Information
Cathay Pacific   ☎ 2747 1234
Air Canada   ☎ 2769 6032
Air New Zealand   ☎ 2842 3642
British Airways   ☎ 2216 1088
Qantas   ☎ 2822 9060
United Airlines   ☎ 2801 8617

Hotel Booking Service
☎ 2286 8888

Left Luggage
☎ 2261 0110

Car Park Information
☎ 2286 0163, 2949 1083

Airport Access

Train The Airport Express connects Chek Lap Kok with Hong Kong Station ($100) in Central, stopping at Tsing Yi ($50) and Kowloon ($80) along the way. The train takes just 23mins to get to the city and runs every 10mins 6am-1am daily. Vending machines (cash only) dispense tickets at the airport and railway stations en route. You can also use Octopus cards (see Travel Passes p. 108).

When leaving Hong Kong, Airport Express stations have check-in counters for flights from Chek Lap Kok, meaning you can check your bags and obtain a boarding pass for your flight before you've even hit the airport. Call ☎ 2881 8888 for more information.

Bus The Airbus is an efficient service, taking 35-45mins. Bus No A21 ($33) is best for Kowloon, with stops along Nathan Rd in Mong Kok, Yau Ma Tei and Tsim Sha Tsui. Bus No A11 ($40) goes to Sheung Wan, Central, Admiralty and Causeway Bay. Change is not given on the bus; tickets can be bought at the booth near the airport bus stand.

Hotel shuttle buses cost $120 and can easily be found in the arrivals hall.

Taxi A taxi to the city centre costs around $350 ($250 to Kowloon). Taxi stands are well signposted.

Bus

Several transport companies in Hong Kong offer bus services to Guangzhou, Shenzhen and several other destinations in Guangdong Province. The best of these is Citybus (☎ 2736 3888), which also operates a domestic bus network in Hong Kong.

Train

The Kowloon-Guangzhou express train, which covers the 182km route in around 2hrs, departs from the Kowloon-Canton Railway (KCR) station in Hung Hom, Kowloon. There are seven departures daily. Tickets can be booked up to seven days in advance at KCR stations in Hung Hom, Mong Kok, Kowloon Tong and Sha Tin, from China Travel Service agents or over the phone (☎ 2947 7888).

There is a direct rail link between Kowloon, Shanghai and Beijing. Trains to Beijing (via Guangzhou, Changsha, Wuchang and Zhengzhou) leave on alternate days, take 30hrs, and cost $574 (hard sleeper), $934 (soft sleeper) and $1191 (deluxe soft sleeper). The trains to Shanghai (via Guangzhou and Hangzhou) also leave on alternate days, take 29 hrs, and cost $508/825/1039. There is also one departure daily to Zhaoqing via Foshan. Call ☎ 2947 7888 for information and tickets.

Boat

Services to/from Macau run virtually 24hrs. Boats depart from the Macau Jetfoil pier (4, B3) at the Shun Tak Centre, 200 Connaught Rd, Sheung Wan, and the China ferry terminal (3, G2), Canton Rd, Kowloon. Tickets ($130 from Hong Kong, $120 from Kowloon; higher prices at night) can be bought at the pier, or over the phone on ☎ 2859 3333. If you're travelling on the weekend, it's advisable to book ahead.

Jet catamarans and hovercraft leave from the China ferry terminal to destinations in neighbouring Guangdong Province, including Huizhou, Nanhai, Shenzhen, Zhuhai and Guangzhou.

Turbo Cat has two trips daily to East River Guangzhou (the Guangzhou Economic Zone); phone ☎ 2851 1700 for more details.

The China ferry terminal also has daily morning jet boats to Wuzhou in Guangxi Province, from where you can link up with buses to Guilin, Yangshuo and Nanning.

Travel Documents

Passport
Must be valid for one month from date of entry.

Visa
Not required for citizens of the UK (up to six months), Commonwealth countries and most Western European countries (up to three months) and Japan and South Africa (up to one month). Others should check visa regulations before leaving home.

Return/Onward Ticket
A return ticket may be required.

Customs

Firearms are strictly controlled and special permits are needed to import them. Meat, plant and textile products are restricted. Pirated copies of computer software or music are banned: this law is aimed at traders but individuals should still be careful.

The duty-free allowance for visitors is 200 cigarettes (or 50 cigars or 250g tobacco) and 1L of alcohol. Apart from these limits there are few other import taxes, so you can bring in reasonable quantities of almost anything.

Departure Tax

Hong Kong levies a departure tax of $50 per person which is usually prepaid when you buy your air ticket.

GETTING AROUND

Hong Kong is small and crowded, and therefore public transport is the only practical way to move people. Consequently public transport is cheap, fast, widely used and generally efficient.

The ultra-modern Mass Transit Railway (MTR) subway is the quickest way to get to most urban destinations. The bus system is extensive and as efficient as traffic allows but it can be bewildering for short-stay travellers. Ferries are fast and cheap and come with bonus harbour views when the weather cooperates.

Travel Passes

The rechargeable **Octopus** card allows you to travel on the MTR, the Airport Express, the KCR East Rail, most cross-harbour bus routes, all outlying islands routes of the Hong Kong Ferry Co (HKF) ferries and some suburban buses. The card costs $150, which includes a $50 refundable deposit and $100 worth of travel. It is available from the ticket offices and customer service centres in MTR, Airport Express and KCR East Rail stations and certain piers of the HKF.

Transport passes aimed at tourists are not good value as you are charged for a 'souvenir' card.

Bus

Kowloon Motor Bus (KMB) buses service Kowloon and the New Territories, while Citybuses cover Hong Kong Island. New World First Buses span the whole territory. Most buses run from about 6am to midnight. Fares range from $2.50 to $30, though a typical trip will cost around $5. Payment is made by Octopus or by depositing cash into a fare box upon entry; no change is given.

In Central, the most important bus station is on the ground floor under Exchange Square (4, D5). From this station you can catch buses to Aberdeen, Repulse Bay, Stanley and other destinations on the south side of Hong Kong Island. In Kowloon, the Star Ferry Bus Station (3, J3) is the most crucial, with buses up Nathan Rd and to the KCR station.

Figuring out which bus you want can be difficult. One useful fact to know is that any bus number ending with the letter M (51M, 68M etc) goes to an MTR station. Buses with an X are express. Bus Nos 121 and 122 are night buses that operate through the Cross-Harbour Tunnel every 15mins from 12.45 to 5am.

Minibus

Known as Public Light Buses, minibuses are cream-coloured with a green or red roof or stripe down the side. These 16-seaters can be handy to go short distances. In Tsim Sha Tsui the No 1 minibus runs from the Star Ferry terminal to Tsim Sha Tsui East every 5mins from 7am to 10pm ($2.50). On Hong Kong Island, a useful route is from Edinburgh Place (near the Star Ferry terminal) to the Peak.

The price to the final destination is displayed on a card propped up in the window. You pay when you get on and no change is given.

Train

The MTR is clean, fast, safe and one of the world's most modern subway systems. Though at between $4 and $13 it costs a bit more than other forms of public transport, it is the quickest way to get to most urban destinations. Trains run every

2 to 4mins, 6am to 1am daily on four lines. Avoid rush hours if possible: 7-9.30am and 5-7pm. Some three million people use the MTR every day, most of them at these times.

Everything is automated, from the ticket vending machines to the turnstiles. Ticket machines take $10, $5, $2, $1 and 50c pieces, and give change; a handful of machines take $20 notes. The easiest way to travel on the MTR is with an Octopus card (see Travel Passes earlier).

The MTR passenger information hotline (☎ 2750 0170) can answer queries.

Kowloon-Canton Railway (KCR)

The KCR is a single-line commuter railway running from Kowloon to the border with mainland China at Lo Wu. The KCR is a quick way to get up to the New Territories, and the ride offers some nice views. The half-hour ride to Sheung Shui costs $9 ($18 for 1st class), while the 45min trip to Lo Wu costs $33 ($66).

A double-decker train speeds from Hung Hom nonstop to Lo Wu. This cuts the journey time by 15mins; tickets are $66. The KCR customer service number is ☎ 2602 7799.

Tram

Hong Kong's double-decker trams are not fast but are cheap and fun. For a flat fare of $2 (dropped in a box beside the driver when you leave) you can rattle along as far as you like, whether it's one block or to the end of the line. Trams operate 6am-1am, and run every 2 to 7mins. Try to get a seat at the front window upstairs to enjoy a first-class view. See p. 18 for more information on Hong Kong trams.

There are eight routes: Kennedy Town to Causeway Bay; Kennedy Town to Happy Valley; Kennedy Town to North Point; Kennedy Town to Shau Kei Wan; Shau Kei Wan to Happy Valley; Western Market to Causeway Bay; Western Market to Shau Kei Wan; and Whitty Street to North Point.

The Peak Tram departs from Garden Rd, near the north-west corner of Hong Kong Park, Admiralty (4, G6). It runs to Victoria Peak every 10 to 15mins from 7am to midnight. The one-way fare is $20 ($30 return); children 3-12 $6/9, seniors $7/14.

Ferry

There are four Star Ferry routes, but by far the most popular is the one running between Tsim Sha Tsui and Central. The trip takes 7mins, and there are frequent departures. Fares for the lower and upper deck are $1.70 and $2.20 respectively. Those 65 years of age and over ride for free. Star ferries also link Tsim Sha Tsui with Wan Chai, and Central with Hung Hom and Discovery Bay (Lantau). See p. 28 for more information on the Star Ferry.

The Hong Kong Ferry (HKF) company connects Hong Kong Island to Kowloon and the New Territories. Useful routes from Central chug to Yau Ma Tei (Jordan Rd) and Tsim Sha Tsui East. HKF also services outlying islands, including Lantau, Cheung Chau, Peng Chau and Lamma Island. Departures are from Piers 6 and 7 (4, C6), west of the Star Ferry pier in Central.

Car

Driving a car in crowded Hong Kong brings little joy. The traffic often slows to a crawl and finding parking is a nightmare.

Road Rules

Driving is on the left side of the road. Seat belts must be worn by the driver and all front-seat passengers in taxis and by front- and back-seat passengers in private cars.

The speed limit is 50km/h in urban areas and up to 100km/h on highways. The blood alcohol limit is 0.05%. Drivers are not permitted to use hand-held mobile phones while in motion.

Rental

Many businesspeople hire cars with drivers – even if you're stuck in traffic, you can skim through notes and make phone calls and you don't have to worry about parking. Ace Hire Car (☎ 2893 0541), 16 Min Fat St, Happy Valley, charges $540/4hrs for a Mercedes Benz with driver. Most hotels will also be able to organise a car for you.

If you're hellbent on driving yourself, Avis (5, G3; ☎ 2890 6988), 93 Leighton Rd, Causeway Bay, charges around $750/day for a compact car. Drivers must be at least 25 years of age.

Driving Licence & Permit

Anyone over the age of 18 with a valid driving licence from their home country or an international driving licence can drive in Hong Kong for up to 12 months.

Motoring Organisations

The Hong Kong Automobile Association (3, B4; ☎ 2739 5273) is at 391 Nathan Rd, Yau Ma Tei.

PRACTICAL INFORMATION

Climate & When to Go

October-November and April-May are probably the best times to visit. Temperatures are moderate, and there's a good chance of clear skies and sun. December-March tends to see a lot of rain, and from June to September the sweltering heat and humidity make for rather sweaty sightseeing.

Hong Kong hotels have two high seasons: March-April and October-November. You can find substantial discounts on accommodation outside these peak demand periods.

Travel in and out of Hong Kong can be difficult during Chinese New Year, which falls around late January/early February.

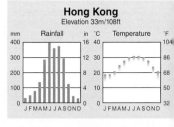

Hong Kong
Elevation 33m/108ft

Tourist Information

Tourist Information Abroad

The Hong Kong Tourist Association (HKTA) is a government-sponsored organisation dedicated to promoting Hong Kong tourism and dealing with any inquiries visitors may have. It produces reams of useful pamphlets and publications and its Web site (www.hkta.org) is a good point of reference. The Association runs an extensive network of overseas offices. Some of these include:

Australia
L4, Hong Kong House, 80 Druitt St, Sydney, NSW 2000 (☎ 02-9283 3083; e hktasyd@hkta.org)

Canada
3rd fl, Hong Kong Trade Centre, 9 Temperance St, Toronto, Ontario M5H 1Y6 (☎ 416-366 2389; e hktayyz@hkta.org)

New Zealand
PO Box 2120, Auckland (☎ 09-307 2580; e hktaauk@hkta.org)

South Africa
c/o Development Promotions Pty Ltd, 7th fl, Everite House, 20 De Korte St, Braamfontein 2001 (☎ 011-339 4865; e hktajnb@hkta.org)

UK
6 Grafton St, London, W1X 3LB (☎ 020-7533 7100; e hktalon@hkta.org)

USA
Suite 1640, 401 N Michigan Ave, Chicago, IL 60611 (☎ 312-329 1828; e hktachi@hkta.org); 2nd fl, 115 E 54th St, New York, NY 10022-4512 (☎ 212-421 3382; e hktanyc@hkta.org); Suite 2050, 10940 Wilshire Blvd, Los Angeles, CA 90024-3915 (☎ 310-208 4582; e hktalax@hkta.org)

Local Tourist Offices
The HKTA has several local offices. You can call the HKTA hotline on ☎ 250 1234 Mon-Fri 8am to 6pm, weekends and holidays 9am to 5pm. There are HKTA offices at the airport (1, E2), Star Ferry Terminal in Tsim Sha Tsui (3, K3), and in The Center, 99 Queen's Rd, Central (4, D4).

Consulates

Hong Kong is one of the world's most consulate-clogged cities.

Australia
23rd & 24th fl, Harbour Centre, 25 Harbour Rd, Wan Chai (4, E13; ☎ 2827 8881)

Canada
11th-14th fl, Tower One, Exchange Square, 8 Connaught Pl, Central (4, D6; ☎ 2810 4321)

New Zealand
6501 Central Plaza, 18 Harbour Rd, Wan Chai (4, F13; ☎ 2525 5044)

South Africa
Great Eagle Centre, 23 Harbour Rd, Wan Chai (4, E13; ☎ 2577 3279)

UK
1 Supreme Court Rd, Admiralty (4, G8; ☎ 2901 3000)

USA
26 Garden Rd, Central (4, G6; ☎ 2523 9011)

Money

Currency
The local currency is the Hong Kong dollar (often expressed as $HK; $ throughout this book). The dollar is divided into 100c. Bills are issued in denominations of $20 (grey), $50 (blue), $100 (red), $500 (brown) and $1000 (yellow). Coins are issued in denominations of 10c, 20c, 50c, $1, $2, $5 and $10.

Travellers Cheques
Most banks cash travellers cheques, but all charge a fee. The best deal is probably the Dao Heng Bank, which charges a flat rate of $20 per cheque. The Hongkong and Shanghai Bank charges 0.375% of the total amount (minimum charge $50), Standard Chartered tacks on a 0.375% (minimum $100) commission and Hang Seng charges $60 an encashment. Licensed money-changers don't levy a commission but give a lower rate of exchange.

Credit Cards
The most widely accepted credit cards in Hong Kong are American Express, Diners Club, JCB, MasterCard and Visa. For 24hr card

cancellations or assistance, call:

American Express
☎ 2885 9366 or 2811 1200

Diners Club
☎ 2860 1888

JCB
☎ 2366 7211

MasterCard
☎ 2598 8038 or 800 966 677

Visa
☎ 2810 8033

ATMs

You will rarely have to search far to find an ATM. International travellers will be able to withdraw funds from their home accounts using just about any cashpoint in town. Refreshingly, most banks do not pilfer a fee for the service.

Changing Money

Licensed moneychangers, such as Thomas Cook and Chequepoint, are abundant in tourist areas like Tsim Sha Tsui and Central. They are open on Sunday, holidays and late into the evenings. There is no commission, but the exchange rates offered are equivalent to a 5% commission.

Banks have marginally better exchange rates. They open Mon-Fri 9am to 4.30pm and Sat 9am to 12.30pm.

Tipping

Although tipping was never customary for the Chinese, westerners have introduced it to Hong Kong. Feel no obligation to tip taxi drivers, but do tip hotel porters at least $10. If you make use of the porters at the airport, $2 a suitcase is normally expected. Hotels and restaurants usually add a 10% service charge. In fancy restaurants customers may tip an extra 5-10% for good service but this isn't obligatory.

Discounts

Children and seniors are routinely offered half-price for transport and attractions but family tickets are not usually available. Museum passes cost $50 – this gets you into all museums for one month.

Student & Youth Cards

If you're a student or you're under 27, you can get an STA Youth Card. Students under 27 qualify for an International Student Identity Card (ISIC), which entitles you to discounts on airfares, trains and museums. To get this card, inquire at your campus.

For Seniors

There are half-price discounts for seniors (65 and over) on buses and ferries, and on MTR and KCR trains. The Star Ferry offers free travel for seniors. There are also discounts for those aged 60 and over in museums and on organised tours. Some upmarket hotels have discounts for seniors, though these can be somewhat bogus because anyone can get good discounts at a hotel by booking through a travel agent.

Travel Insurance

A policy which covers theft, loss, medical expenses and compensation for cancellation or delays in your travel arrangements is highly recommended. If items are lost or stolen, make sure you get a police report straight away otherwise your insurer might not pay up.

Opening Hours

Business hours are Mon-Fri 9am to 5 or 6pm, and Sat 9am to noon. Many offices close for lunch between 1 and 2pm. Stores that cater to the tourist trade keep longer hours, but almost nothing opens before 9am and many stores don't open till 10 or 11am. Even tourist-related businesses shut down by 10pm. Most post offices are open Mon-Fri 8am to 6pm, Sat until 2pm, and are closed on Sunday and public holidays.

Most banks and shops are closed on public holidays, especially Chinese New Year, while restaurants usually keep Sunday hours. Museums and other attractions may close on Christmas and Boxing days.

Public Holidays

Jan	New Year's Day (1st weekday in Jan)
Jan/Feb	Chinese New Year (3 days)
Late Mar/Apr	Easter (3 days)
Early April	Ching Ming
Late April	Buddha's Birthday
1 May	Labour Day
Late June	Tuen Ng Festival
1 July	Hong Kong SAR Establishment Day
1 Oct	National Day
Early Oct	Chinese Mid-Autumn Festival
Late Oct	Cheung Yeung
25 Dec	Christmas Day
26 Dec	Boxing Day

Time

Hong Kong Standard Time is 8hrs ahead of GMT/UTC and summer/daylight-savings time isn't practised. At noon in Hong Kong it's:

11pm the previous day in New York
8pm the previous day in Los Angeles
4am in London
noon in Singapore, Manila and Perth
2pm in Melbourne and Sydney

Electricity

The standard voltage is 220V, 50Hz (cycles per second) AC. Most electric outlets are designed for three square pins of the British design; others are wired to accommodate three round prongs and others for two prong plugs! Not surprisingly, inexpensive plug adaptors are widely available.

Weights & Measures

Although the international metric system (see p. 121) is in official use in Hong Kong, in practice traditional Chinese weights and measures are still common. At local markets, things are sold by the *leung*, which is equivalent to 37.8g, and the *gan* (catty), where one gan is about 600g. There are 16 leung to the gan.

Post

On Hong Kong Island, the General Post Office (GPO) is on your right as you disembark from the Star Ferry (3, K3). In addition to standard post office opening hours (see earlier), it opens Sunday 8am-2pm. In Kowloon the most convenient post offices are at 10 Middle Rd (3, J5) behind the Sheraton, and in the basement of Albion Plaza, 2-6 Granville Rd, just off Nathan Rd, Tsim Sha Tsui (3, G5). Most post offices have stamp vending machines outside which are useful after hours. The inquiry number for postal services is ☎ 2921 2222.

Sending Mail

Allow five days for delivery of letters, postcards and aerogrammes to the UK, USA and Australia. Speedpost reduces delivery time by about half.

Postal Rates

Airmail letters and postcards are $2.50 (to Asia except Japan) and $3.10 (elsewhere) for the first 10g; and $1.20 and $1.30 respectively for each additional 10g. Aerogrammes are $2.30 for both zones.

Telephone

All calls made within Hong Kong are local calls and therefore free, except at public pay phones which cost $1 a call. Pay phones accept $1, $2 and $5 coins. You can place an International Direct Dialling (IDD) call from most phone boxes, but you'll probably need a phonecard, which can be bought at Hongkong Telecom shops and 7-Eleven convenience stores.

Lonely Planet's eKno Communication Card, specifically aimed at travellers, provides competitive international calls (avoid using it for local calls), messaging services and free email. Logon to www.ekno.lonelyplanet.com for information on joining and accessing the service.

Mobile Phones

Hong Kong boasts the world's highest per-capita usage of mobile telephones and pagers – they're everywhere, even in road tunnels and the underground railway. Any GSM-compatible phone can be used in Hong Kong.

Hongkong Telecom shops rent and sell mobile phones, SIM cards and phone accessories. SIM cards cost $200, network rental is $200/week and local calls cost $2.20/min. These phones are IDD compatible but there's an extra charge if you need a roaming service to take into China. Handset rentals are available for an extra $250/week.

If you're in Hong Kong for more than two weeks it may be cheaper to buy a phone and network package. Shop around: Hong Kong's mobile phone service providers all work on a knife edge.

There are Hongkong Telecom shops on Level 7 at the airport (7am-11pm); Amtel Bldg, 161-163 Des Voeux Rd, Central (4, C4; 9am-7pm); and 21 Granville Rd, Tsim Sha Tsui, Kowloon (3, F5; 10am-10pm). The customer service hotline is ☎ 2883 3938; faxback information is available from ☎ 2911 1783; and there's a pile of information on HK Telecom's Web site at www.1010.cwhkt.com.

Country/City Code

Hong Kong	☎ 852

Useful Numbers

Directory Inquiries	☎ 1081
International Dialling Code	☎ 001
Int. Fax Dialling Code	☎ 002
Int. Directory Inquiries	☎ 10015
International Operator	☎ 10010
Int. Operator (credit card calls)	☎ 10011
Reverse-Charge (collect)	☎ 10010
Time & Weather	☎ 18501

International Direct Dial Codes

Australia	☎ 001 61
Canada	☎ 001 1
Rest of China	☎ 001 86
Japan	☎ 001 81
New Zealand	☎ 001 64
South Africa	☎ 001 27
United Kingdom	☎ 001 44
USA	☎ 001 1

Email/www

As you'd expect from a community of techno-fiends, the Internet is very popular in Hong Kong. Anything bigger than a ma-and-pa business is likely to have a Web site and just about anyone you're likely to do business with will be contactable by email.

Internet Service Providers

Well-trafficked local ISPs include Hongkong Telecom's Netvigator (☎ 183 3888) and HKNet (☎ 2110 2288; ⓔ info@hknet.com). America Online's customer service number is ☎ 2916 6888.

Internet Cafes

If you can't access the Internet from your hotel, Hong Kong has plenty of cybercafes. In most places the Internet is free if you buy a drink or snack. This sort of service is great but it can mean lengthy queues, both those you have to wait in and those breathing down your neck.

Pacific Coffee Company
    1st fl, International Finance Centre, 1 Harbour View St (4, D6; ☎ 2868 5100; free with drink); also Times Sq and most other malls

Cash Online
    Shop 1b, Haiphong Mansion, 99-101 Nathan Rd, Tsim Sha Tsui (3, G5; ☎ 2366 0030; free with drink); also at Shop 9-12, Excelsior Plaza, 24-26 East Point Plaza, Causeway Bay (5, F3; ☎ 2972 2068)

i-Cable Station
    2nd fl, Shop 205-205a, Ocean Terminal, Harbour City, Tsim Tsa Shui (3, J2; ☎ 2537 8778)

Kublai's
    3rd fl, One Capital Pl, 18 Luard Rd, Wan Chai (4, F12; ☎ 2529 9117; $48/30mins); also at 55 Kimberley Rd, Tsim Sha Tsui (3, F6; ☎ 2722 0733)

Useful Sites

The Lonely Planet Web site (www.lonelyplanet.com) links to Hong Kong sites via SubWWWay and covers travel news at Scoop. Other useful sites include:

Hong Kong Tourist Association
    www.hkta.org

South China Morning Post (news)
    www.scmp.com.hk

Totally Hong Kong (lifestyle)
    www.totallyhk.com

Yellow Pages
    www.yp.com.hk

Hong Kong government information
    www.info.gov.hk

Doing Business

The Hong Kong Trade Development Council (TDC) promotes Hong Kong as a trading and manufacturing partner for foreign businesses. Facilities in its topnotch office within the Convention & Exhibition Centre include a library (4, E12; ☎ 2584 4333) where you can access trade statistics and information about business and economic trends.

Another source for trade information, statistics, government regulations and product certification is the Hong Kong Trade Department (2, B2; ☎ 2392 2922), Trade Department Tower, 700 Nathan Rd, Mong Kok. The Hong Kong Industry Department (3, H3; ☎ 2737 2208), 14th fl, Ocean Centre, 5 Canton Rd, Tsim Sha Tsui, offers information and assistance to overseas investors . Female movers and shakers could find the Women Business Owners Club (☎ 2541 0446) useful for tips and contacts.

If you need to rent office space try Asia Pacific Business Centre (4, F8; ☎ 2530 8888; fax 2530 8100; e asiapac@winclient.com), 2207-9 Tower 2, Lippo Centre, Admiralty or Central Executive Business Centre (4, E5; ☎ 2841 7888; fax 2810 1868), 11th fl, Central Bldg, 1 Pedder St, Central. Both rent offices daily, weekly and monthly and have multilingual office support staff on hand. They also offer telephone answering and message taking services. Expect to pay from $600/day ($2400/week).

Polyglot Translations (6, B2; ☎ 2851 7232; fax 2545 9537; e polyglot@hkstar.com), 14b Time Centre, 53 Hollywood Rd, Central, offers translation and interpretation services. English-Cantonese document translation costs $1.40/word ($500 minimum), while simultaneous interpretation costs $5900/day and consecutive interpretation costs $5000/day or $625/hr with a minimum of 4hrs.

Newspapers & Magazines

The local English-language dailies are the *South China Morning Post* and *i-Mail* (Mon-Sat), which has replaced the old *Hong Kong Standard*. The mouthpiece *China Daily* prints a Hong Kong edition.

Asian editions of the *Asian Wall Street Journal*, *USA Today* and the *International Herald Tribune* are printed in Hong Kong. Hotel bookshops are the best places to find overseas newspapers and magazines.

Radio

Hong Kong's most popular English-language radio stations are RTHK Radio 3 (567AM, 1584AM, 97.9FM, 106.8FM); RTHK Radio 4 (classical music, 98.9FM); RTHK Radio 6 (BBC World Service 675AM); Commercial Radio (864AM); Metro News (1044AM); Hit Radio (99.7FM); FM Select (104FM); and Quote AM (alternative and dance music, 864AM). The South China Morning Post publishes a daily guide to radio programs.

TV

Hong Kong's terrestrial TV stations are run by two companies, Television Broadcasts (TVB) and Asia Television (ATV). They each run one English-language and one Cantonese-language channel. The two English stations are TVB Pearl (channel 3) and ATV World (channel 4). The two Cantonese stations are TVB Jade (channel 1) and ATV Home (channel 2). The program schedule is listed daily in the *South China Morning Post* and in a weekly Sunday liftout.

Photography & Video

Almost everything you could possibly need in the way of photographic accessories is available in Hong Kong. Stanley St on Hong Kong Island is the place to look for reputable camera stores (see Shopping, p. 64).

Hong Kong subscribes to the PAL video standard used in Australia, New Zealand, UK and most of Europe. It is incompatible with SECAM (used in France and Germany) and NTSC (Canada, Japan, Korea, Latin America and USA).

Health

Immunisations

There are no specific vaccination requirements for Hong Kong or Macau. For Guangzhou and southern China, a yellow fever vaccination is needed if you are coming from a yellow fever infected area.

Precautions

In general, health conditions in Hong Kong are good. The government insists that Hong Kong's tap water is perfectly safe to drink and does not need to be boiled. However, most local Chinese boil it anyway, more out of habit than necessity. Bottled water is widely available.

Practice the usual precautions when it comes to sex; condoms are available in convenience stores, pharmacies and supermarkets.

Insurance & Medical Treatment

Although you may have medical insurance in your own country, it is probably not valid in Hong Kong; check before you leave. Travel insurance is advisable to cover any medical treatment you may need while in Hong Kong. Medical care is of a high standard though public hospital staff and facilities are stretched. Private hospital treatment is expensive, but not exorbitant and you'll have less of a wait for treatment.

Medical Services

The general inquiry number for hospitals is ☎ 2300 6555. Some hospitals with 24hr accident and emergency departments include:

Queen Elizabeth Hospital (public)
  30 Gascoigne Rd, Yau Ma Tei, Kowloon (3, A6; ☎ 2958 8888)

Queen Mary Hospital (public)
  102 Pok Fu Lam Rd, Pok Fu Lam, Hong Kong Island (2, D2; ☎ 2855 3111)

Hong Kong Central (private)
  1b Lower Albert Rd, Central, Hong Kong Island 6, E5; ☎ 2522 3141)

Dental Services

Private dental clinics can be found throughout Hong Kong; hospitals also offer emergency dental services. To find a dentist nearby, ask your hotel or call the Dental Council (☎ 2873 5862).

Pharmacies

Mannings and Watson's are the two main pharmacy chains with branches in every shopping centre and dozens of street frontage outlets. Most are open until 10pm. The hospitals listed above have dispensing chemists on duty 24hrs.

Traditional Practitioners

Traditional Chinese medicine is extremely popular in Hong Kong, both as a preventative and curative. Probably the most famous practice is Eu Yan Sang (6, A3; ☎ 2544 3870), 152-156 Queen's Rd, Central. The doctors speak good English if you want a consultation. The store is also an interesting place to browse as many of the healing ingredients are displayed and explained.

Toilets

You need a strong bladder to visit Hong Kong – the city suffers from a scarcity of public toilets. All shopping malls have toilets, but may keep most doors locked so only employees with keys can use them. You can seek out toilets in hotels, fast-food outlets (though not all have them) and in some of the large department stores.

Safety Concerns

Hong Kong is extremely safe for visitors. You can travel on public transport and walk city streets until late at night with very low risk of being harassed. As you go further north in Kowloon and into the New Territories, the crime rate increases somewhat, but criminals would still rather target locals than visitors.

Signs warn against pickpockets but incidents of theft are relatively rare. In any event, it's unwise to flash valuables and you should remain alert.

Lost Property

Each public transport service in the city manages their own lost property, so even if you can't remember to take your bag with you, remember which bus you left it on!

Citybus	☎ 2873 0818
Hongkong Tramways	☎ 2559 8918
Hongkong Ferry	☎ 2542 3081
KCR	☎ 2602 7799
KMB	☎ 2745 4466
MTR	☎ 2881 8888
New World First Bus	☎ 2136 8888
Peak Tramways	☎ 2522 0922
Star Ferry	☎ 2366 2576

Keeping Copies

Make photocopies of all your important documents, keep some with you, separate from the originals, and leave a copy at home. You can also store details of documents in Lonely Planet's free online Travel Vault, password-protected and accessible worldwide (www.ekno.lonelyplanet.com).

Emergency Numbers

Ambulance	☎ 999
Fire	☎ 999
Police	☎ 999
Police (non-emergency)	☎ 2527 7177
Rape Crisis Line	☎ 2522 0434

Women Travellers

Principles of decorum and respect for women are deeply ingrained in Chinese culture. Despite the Confucianist sense of superiority accorded men, Chinese women often call the shots and wield a tremendous amount of influence (especially within marriage). There is a strong sense of balance between men and women in Hong Kong.

The experience of most women travellers is that Hong Kong is a safe city. Few complain of bad treatment, intimidation or aggression, and for the most part your experience should be hassle-free. That said, it is still important to keep your wits about you, especially if you're wandering about alone at night. You should also be wary of agencies seeking western women to work as models, escorts and extras in films; these agencies can be fronts for prostitution.

Tampons are widely available but there's not a lot of variety – most Hong Kong women use pads. The contraceptive pill is available by prescription.

Gay & Lesbian Travellers

The PRC's official attitude to gays and lesbians in mainland China is ambiguous, with responses ranging from draconian penalties to tacit acceptance. In Hong Kong the official attitude is far more positive. In July 1991 the enactment of the Crimes (Amendment) Ordinance removed criminal penalties for homosexual acts between male adults. Since the amendment, gay groups have been lobbying for anti-discrimination legislation to address the issue of discrimination on the grounds of sexual orientation. Despite this apparent liberalisation, Hong Kong Chinese are fairly conservative and it can still be risky for gays and lesbians to 'come out' to family or employers.

The gay scene in Hong Kong has seen a small revolution take place over the past few years. See page 89 for listings.

Information & Organisations

Horizons (☎ 2815 9268) is a volunteer-run switchboard service offering advice to local and visiting gays, lesbians and bisexuals. See www.gaystation.com.hk for nightlife info and gay radio broadcasts.

Senior Travellers

With decent medical care, pharmacies, air conditioning and good public transport, Hong Kong offers most of the usual modern conveniences that make travel safe and comfortable. However, some senior travellers may have difficulty negotiating the steep hills or the steps on pedestrian overpasses and in the MTR stations. Senior discounts are available; see page 112.

Information

The Hong Kong Society for the

Aged (4, F13; ☎ 2511 2235), Rm1601, Tung Sun Commercial Centre, 194 Lockhart Rd, Wan Chai, deals with issues relating to the elderly.

Disabled Travellers

Disabled people will have to cope with substantial obstacles in Hong Kong, such as the stairs at the MTR stations, narrow crowded footpaths and steep hills. People whose sight, hearing or walking ability is impaired must be extremely cautious of Hong Kong's crazy drivers, who almost never yield to pedestrians. Crossing busy thoroughfares on pedestrian overpasses will also be a problem for some disabled travellers.

On the other hand, taxis are not hard to find and most buildings have lifts. Wheelchairs can negotiate most of the ferries (lower deck only). Some newer buses can take wheelchairs.

Some hotels have specially designed rooms for disabled guests. Chek Lap Kok airport has good facilities for special needs passengers: a free porter service is available, numerous ramps make moving between levels simple and lifts are equipped with audible indicators.

Information & Organisations

The tourist association publishes a booklet listing which of Hong Kong's hotels, attractions and shopping centres cater to wheelchair visitors. The Joint Council for the Physically and Mentally Disabled (☎ 2864 2931; fax 2864 2962) might be able to help.

Language

Hong Kong's two official languages are English and Cantonese. However, around 70% of the population of China speaks the Beijing dialect (commonly known as Mandarin) which is the official language of the People's Republic of China (PRC).

While Cantonese is used in Hong Kong in everyday life, English is still the primary language of commerce, banking and international trade, and is also used in the higher law courts.

Since the handover, there has been a sharp rise in Mandarin-speaking tourists and some locals are now learning Mandarin, instead of English, as their second language. Still, short-term English-speaking visitors can get along fine in Hong Kong without a word of Cantonese, especially in the tourist zones. Street signs and public transport information are presented in both English and Cantonese, so there's no problem getting around. However, in the back streets, markets and non-touristy restaurants, conversing with locals will be more difficult.

Tones & Romanisation

Chinese languages have many homonyms (sound-alike words). What distinguishes the meaning of these words are changes in a speaker's pitch (tones) and the context of the word within the sentence. Attempting to explain the tonal system (or the various Romanisation systems used to render Cantonese script into a form westerners can read and pronounce) would require a disordinate amount of space. The words and phrases included here therefore use a simplified Romanisation system and are not marked for tones.

For an in depth guide to Cantonese – with loads of useful information on grammar, tones and pronunciation, together with a comprehensive phrase list – get a copy of Lonely Planet's *Cantonese phrasebook*.

Basics

Hello, how are you?	*nei ho?*
I'm fine.	*ngoh gei ho*
Good morning.	*jo san*
Goodbye.	*baai baai*
Goodnight.	*jo tau*
Thank you.	*doh je*
You're welcome.	*m sai haak hei*
Excuse me.	*m goi*
I'm sorry.	*dui m jue*
My surname is ...	*siu sing ...*
My name is ...	*ngoh giu jo ...*
Do you speak English?	*nei sik m sik gong ying man a?*
I (don't) understand.	*ngoh (m) ming baak*

Getting Around

Go straight ahead.	*yat jik hui*
left/right	*joh bin/yau bin*
bus stop	*ba si jaam*
ferry pier	*siu lin ma tau*
subway station	*dei tit jaam*
information centre	*sun man chue*
I'd like to go to ...	*ngoh seung hui ...*
Does this (bus) go to ...?	*ni ga (ba si) hui m hui ... a?*
Where is the ..., please?	*cheng man ... hai bin do a?*
Is it far?	*yuen m yuen a?*
Please write down the address for me.	*m goi se goh dei ji bei ngoh*

Accommodation

Do you have any rooms?	*yau mo fong a?*
I'd like a (single/double) room.	*ngoh seung yiu yat goh (daan/seung) yan fong*
How much per night?	*gei doh chin yat maan a?*

Eating & Drinking

restaurant	*chaan teng*
bar	*jau ba*
food court/street	*sik gaai*
I'm a vegetarian.	*ngoh hai so sik ge*
Do you have an English menu?	*yau mo ying man chaan paai a?*
I'd like the set menu, please.	*ngoh yiu goh to chaan*
Please bring me (a knife and fork).	*m goi loh (yat fooh do cha) bei ngoh*
Please bring the bill.	*m goi maai daan*

Shopping

How much is this?	*ni goh geih doh chin a?*
Can you reduce the price?	*pehng di dak m dak a?*

Days & Numbers

today	*gam yat*
tomorrow	*ting yat*
yesterday	*kam yat*
0	*ling*
1	*yat*
2	*yi* (or *lehung*)
3	*saam*
4	*sei*
5	*ng*
6	*luk*
7	*chat*
8	*baat*
9	*gau*
10	*sap*
11	*sap yat*
12	*sap yi*
20	*yi sap*
21	*yi sap yat*
100	*yat baak*
1000	*yat chin*
10,000	*yat maan*

Health & Emergencies

Help!	*gau meng a!*
Call the police!	*giu ging chaat!*
I'm sick.	*ngoh yau beng*
I need a doctor.	*ngoh sui yiu yat wai ge yi sang*

Conversion Table

Clothing Sizes

Measurements approximate only; try before you buy.

Women's Clothing

Aust/NZ	8	10	12	14	16	18
Europe	36	38	40	42	44	46
Japan	5	7	9	11	13	15
UK	8	10	12	14	16	18
USA	6	8	10	12	14	16

Women's Shoes

Aust/NZ	5	6	7	8	9	10
Europe	35	36	37	38	39	40
France only	35	36	38	39	40	42
Japan	22	23	24	25	26	27
UK	3½	4½	5½	6½	7½	8½
USA	5	6	7	8	9	10

Men's Clothing

Aust/NZ	92	96	100	104	108	112
Europe	46	48	50	52	54	56
Japan	S		M	M		L
UK	35	36	37	38	39	40
USA	35	36	37	38	39	40

Men's Shirts (Collar Sizes)

Aust/NZ	38	39	40	41	42	43
Europe	38	39	40	41	42	43
Japan	38	39	40	41	42	43
UK	15	15½	16	16½	17	17½
USA	15	15½	16	16½	17	17½

Men's Shoes

Aust/NZ	7	8	9	10	11	12
Europe	41	42	43	44½	46	47
Japan	26	27	27.5	28	29	30
UK	7	8	9	10	11	12
USA	7½	8½	9½	10½	11½	12½

Weights & Measures

Length & Distance

1 inch = 2.54cm
1cm = 0.39 inches
1m = 3.3ft
1ft = 0.3m
1km = 0.62 miles
1 mile = 1.6km

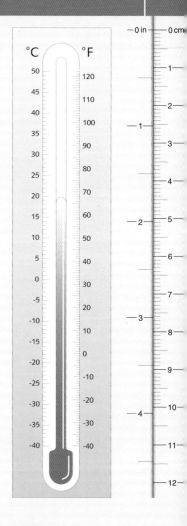

Weight

1kg = 2.2lb
1lb = 0.45kg
1g = 0.04oz
1oz = 28g

Volume

1 litre = 0.26 US gallons
1 US gallon = 3.8 litres
1 litre = 0.22 imperial gallons
1 imperial gallon = 4.55 litres

THE AUTHOR

Dani Valent

Dani Valent has been writing Lonely Planet guides since 1995. She's travelled from A to Z via B, C, T, W and the MCG in the process. For this Hong Kong jaunt, she packed chopsticks, sandals, an umbrella and a flotilla of handheld computing devices. Her favourite thing about this trip to not-quite-China? The demise of the gnarly neighbourhood runway at the old Kai Tak airport! When back home in Melbourne (it's south of Sydney), Australia, Dani spends time with her fish, Kouta and Tugga, and her two snails (both called Petal).

Thanks to: Mandy Lo, Liam Fitzpatrick and all at HKTA, Matt Pirrie, Jeannie Hau, John Batten, Lamey Chang, Vincent Chui, Isabel Ho, Julie Gaw, Clare Stewart, Stephanie Borland and Ian Strachan.

ABOUT THIS BOOK

Maps by Charles Rawlings-Way • Edited by Anne Mulvaney and Gabrielle Green • Design by James Hardy • Publishing Manager Mary Neighbour • Cover by Daniel New • Thanks to Andrew Weatherill, Andrew Tudor, Diana Saad, Gerard Walker, Glenn Beanland, Lisa Borg, Martin Heng, Quentin Frayne and Richard I'Anson.

OTHER CONDENSED GUIDES

Other Lonely Planet Condensed guides include: *Amsterdam, Boston* (due April 2001), *California, Crete, Frankfurt, London, New York City, Paris, Rome* (due July 2001) and *Sydney*.

ABOUT LONELY PLANET

The story begins with a classic travel adventure: Tony and Maureen Wheeler's 1972 journey across Europe and Asia to Australia. Useful information about the overland trail did not exist at that time, so Tony and Maureen published the first Lonely Planet guidebook to meet a growing need.

From a kitchen table, then from a tiny office in Melbourne, Australia, Lonely Planet has become the largest independent travel publisher in the world, an international company with offices in Melbourne, Oakland (USA), London (UK) and Paris (France).

Today there are over 400 titles, including travel guides, city maps, cycling guides, first time travel guides, healthy travel guides, travel atlases, diving guides, pictorial books, phrasebooks, restaurant guides, travel literature, walking guides watching wildlife and world food guides.

At Lonely Planet we believe that travellers can make a positive contribution to the countries they visit – if they respect their host communities and spend their money wisely. Since 1986 a percentage of the income from books has been donated to aid and human rights projects.

LONELY PLANET ONLINE

www.lonelyplanet.com or AOL keyword: lp
Lonely Planet's award-winning Web site has insider info on hundreds of destinations from Amsterdam to Zimbabwe, complete with interactive maps and colour photographs. You'll also find the latest travel news, recent reports from travellers on the road, guidebook upgrades and a lively bulletin board where you can meet fellow travellers, swap recommendations and seek advice.

PLANET TALK

Our FREE quarterly printed newsletter is full of tips from travellers and anecdotes from Lonely Planet authors. Every issue is packed with up-to-date travel news and advice, and includes a postcard from Lonely Planet co-founder Tony Wheeler, mail from travellers, a look at life on the road through the eyes of a Lonely Planet author, topical health advice, prizes for the best travel yarn, news about forthcoming Lonely Planet events and a complete list of Lonely Planet books and products.

To join our mailing list, email us at: go@lonelyplanet.co.uk (UK, Europe and Africa residents); info@lonelyplanet.com (North and South America residents); talk2us@lonelyplanet.com.au (the rest of the world); or contact any Lonely Planet office.

COMET

Our FREE monthly email newsletter brings you all the latest travel news, features, interviews, competitions, destination ideas, travellers' tips & tales, Q&As, raging debates and related links. Find out what's new on the Lonely Planet Web site and which books are about to hit the shelves.

Subscribe from your desktop: www.lonelyplanet.com/comet

LONELY PLANET OFFICES

Australia
90 Maribyrnong St, Footscray, Vic 3011
☎ 03 9689 4666 fax 03 9680 6833
email: talk2us@lonelyplanet.com.au

UK
10a Spring Place, London NW5 3BH
☎ 020 7428 4800 fax 020 7428 4828
email: go@lonelyplanet.co.uk

USA
150 Linden St, Oakland, CA 94607
☎ 510 893 8555 TOLL FREE: 800 275 8555
fax 510 893 8572
email: info@lonelyplanet.com

France
1 rue du Dahomey, 75011 Paris
☎ 01 55 25 33 00 fax 01 55 25 33 01
email: bip@lonelyplanet.fr
minitel: 3615 lonelyplanet

World Wide Web: www.lonelyplanet.com or AOL keyword: lp
Lonely Planet Images: lpi@lonelyplanet.com.au

index

See separate indexes for Places to Eat (p. 126), Places to Stay (p. 127), Shops (p. 127) and Sights (p. 128, includes map references).

PLACES TO EAT

PLACES TO STAY

SHOPS

sights – quick index